"Finally a book that gets it! Growth requires great people, period. *The Unstoppable Organization* highlights the specific strategies and case studies of the fastest growing organizations from around the world proving that employees who can connect and collaborate with customers, drive the best results. If you are looking for ideas on how to help your organization to grow, this book is a must read!"

—Colleen Francis, author, *Nonstop Sales Boom*

"We've all heard it said that a company's most important asset is its people. When we say we love a company, what we're really saying is we love the work being done by the people in that organization. That's why Shawn Casemore's *The Unstoppable Organization* is so important. He guides you in fostering a culture that empowers employees to deliver lasting value. Following his advice will help you develop an unstoppable group of talented people who do outstanding work. Your customers will be well served and you'll be richly rewarded with exponential growth."

—Scott Wintrip, author, *High Velocity Hiring*

"Another great book from Shawn full of practical strategies for organizations on how to grow and become more profitable."

—Mike Vokes, president, Vokes Furniture Inc.

THE

UNSTOPPABLE ORGANIZATION

EMPOWER YOUR PEOPLE, ENGAGE YOUR CUSTOMERS, AND GROW YOUR REVENUE

SHAWN CASEMORE

CAREER PRESS

The Career Press, Inc.
Wayne, NJ

THE UNSTOPPABLE ORGANIZATION
EDITED BY ROGER SHEETY
TYPESET BY PERFECTYPE, NASHVILLE, TENNESSEE
Cover design by Rob Johnson/toprotype
Wrecking ball image by Kostsov/shutterstock
Printed in the U.S.A.

To order this title, please call toll-free 1-800-CAREER-1 (NJ and Canada: 201-848-0310) to order using VISA or MasterCard, or for further information on books from Career Press.

The Career Press, Inc.
12 Parish Drive
Wayne, NJ 07470
www.careerpress.com

Library of Congress Cataloging-in-Publication Data

CIP Data Available Upon Request.

CONTENTS

Part 3: How to Empower Your Organization to Grow

Part 4: Growing Forward

FOREWORD

D o you know the best way to empower your people, engage your customers, and grow your topline revenue? Even if you think you do, you'll find no better insights into creating an unstoppable organization than in this wonderful book by Shawn Casemore.

In the 15 chapters of *The Unstoppable Organization: Empower Your People, Engage Your Customers, and Grow Your Revenue*, Shawn provides tips, tools, and proven strategies for leaders including providing value, engaging employees online, and empowering your customers and employees to support topline growth.

Shawn starts by deconstructing everything we knew and have been taught about organizational growth. This is quite a beginning to a sometimes personal, sometimes professional treatise to what it is to be a leader in business today.

Throughout the book, Shawn asks us to answer important questions, the result of which will determine the ultimate success or failure of our organizations, for instance: "How can we avoid becoming enamored with the latest and greatest technology, forgetting about the importance of our people?" This is one of those questions that you can bring to your teams and have each member provide answers they believe to be true. Bring all of those answers together and you may be able to combat "forgetting about the importance of people."

This is just one of the great insights you'll find in Shawn's book. Read it, learn from it, and discover what it takes to be a future-ready leader in an unstoppable organization!

Life is good.

—Marshall Goldsmith

Marshall Goldsmith is the international best-selling author and editor of 36 books, including What Got You Here Won't Get You There *and* Triggers.

7

INTRODUCTION

Since the dawn of time when traders peddled their wares in exchange for other goods or money, those who own and lead businesses, from the local variety store owner to the head of a multinational corporation, have been attempting to unlock the secrets to growing their business, steadily increasing their sales revenue through time and consistently capturing market share from their competition. Having worked with executives from across North America, I find that this obsession with growth remains an unlocked mystery for most, which sent me on a quest in search of answers. What I learned throughout my nearly 10-year research is that the *secret* to growth was available to all organizations, but less obvious to most. The so-called experts who promote themselves as holding the secret to growth suggest it is tied directly to an organization's ability to market and sell its products or services effectively. More specifically, in instances where an organization has a great marketing campaign aligned with a strong brand promise and is, in turn, supported by strong selling systems to capitalize on the marketing investment, growth is touted as not only obtainable but perceivably unstoppable.

Interestingly, these same experts often suggest that their own specific process, product, or service is necessary to unlock unstoppable growth for your organization as long as the business owner or executive is willing to unlock their wallet. However, it would appear from nearly a decade of meeting, working with, and supporting CEOs from around North America that this promise is all too often not the magic pill to unstoppable growth, leaving the perceivably elusive question as to what exactly does an organization need to do to become unstoppable? This isn't to say that companies aren't experiencing revenue growth or increased market share, but in the feedback I've received it's often unpredictable and unreliable, making growth more of a roller-coaster ride rather than a slow climb to the top. Growth in one quarter, for example, might be followed by several quarters with lackluster sales. It would seem that not only do these proposed systems and technologies recommended by the experts *not* achieve the results suggested, but they add further complexity to a sales and revenue cycle that is becoming more unpredictable.

When I wrote my first book, *Operational Empowerment: Collaborate, Innovate, and Engage to Beat the Competition,* I wanted to help CEOs, executives, and leaders around the world find and apply the tools that are readily at their finger tips in order to build a stronger performing organization, no experts necessary. In that book, I dedicated several chapters to discussing the important role employees hold in helping to grow and sustain a business and a single chapter sharing examples and practices to identify how employees can support growth in relation to sales, marketing, and customer service. I realize now that a single chapter was not near enough to raise awareness of this opportunity most organizations have because before you ever worry about building a strong performing organization and team (which my first book was written to define), it's critical to first make sales in order to grow the business itself. There is no sense perfecting your operating model if you first can't attract and retain customers to bring in consistently growing revenue.

This book, *The Unstoppable Organization: Empower Your People, Engage Your Customers, and Grow Your Revenue,* was written to overcome my mistake and make things right. I want you to not only know but also understand and apply the not-so secrets of success that some of the fastest growing organizations across North America are using, because this is success that you can have as well. One of the benefits of having been a consultant during the last decade of my career is that it has allowed me to connect with literally hundreds of CEOs and executives to learn about their own unique best practices for growth, practices that are not based on one proposed method or a single proprietary system recommended by an expert, but practical and often overlooked opportunities that have supported growth. This book culminates these best practices that I've heard of, learned, and even applied with clients as a consultant through interventions in which we deconstruct how they approach their market and customers, creating a more powerful engine that will not only grow market share, but also create a repeatable and powerful engine for consistent growth. This isn't about a single process or solution, but rather a culmination of shifts and adjustments in how an organization interacts with customers and employees and how, in turn, this influences growth.

You might be thinking: if this information is so common and practical that it can be documented here, how could you as a business owner, executive, or business leader have missed it? Well, to answer this I want to share a simple example of a client of mine, Saje Natural Wellness. Twenty-five years ago, Kate Ross LeBlanc and Jean-Pierre LeBlanc, the founders of Saje Natural wellness, shared a passion and vision that started them on a journey toward global wellness and building a globally recognized brand. Seeking healthier, more effective, and natural solutions to pharmaceutical medicine, they leveraged Jean-Pierre's background in chemistry and Kate's lifelong love for retail, including a natural talent for design and "everything beautiful," to blend and bring essential oil remedies to the world. Almost three decades later, Kate's original customer service pledge and their commitment to 100 percent natural formulations remain the founding pillars of the company. This customer-centric approach and commitment to the natural has built an unstoppable organization. Before we go any further, let me point out that the fact they've grown in both areas simultaneously is an accomplishment unto itself that few organizations have been able to achieve. Even Amazon, after dominating online, is only now beginning to consider creating a brick and mortar presence, most recently in the grocery sector as of this writing.

But in speaking with Kate to better understand their "secret" formula to such explosive and consistent growth, one thing stands out above all else. The success of Saje is the direct result of the highly talented employees that embrace and live the Saje brand. I know, that sounds like an overwhelmingly simple statement, but in Kate's eyes the success of their organization, from developing their unique products to supporting their global clientele, and even down to identifying new markets to enter, comes back to engaging with her people. What Kate and Jean-Pierre have realized from the start is that a successful organization is built on a successful team, and that this requires more than just hiring experts in their field or holding periodic team-building events. In fact, the key to Saje finding and building their team has been in identifying candidates that are a "fit" within the culture of Saje, more so than having a specific skill set or level of experience. Experience is important, but being able to work well with the Saje team is the driving force behind determining whether you are hired to work for Saje.

There is more to Saje's story and we'll get into this shortly, but I wanted to share this specific example with you because it is rare. In all the years I've been meeting with executives and business owners attempting to unlock the secrets to organizational success, it's rare that the primary consideration is to hire based on "fit within the culture" and "person-ality" over skill. After all, revenue growth, one would surmise, comes from strong marketing, better selling, and high levels of productivity. Interestingly, although these are key components to growth, what I've found is that the primary consideration for organizations that are unstop-pable when it comes to growing is not skills, but rather culture. Though this isn't a primary consideration for most, there has rarely been a CEO who has disagreed with me when I suggest that finding the "right person" who "fits" within a team is often more difficult than finding an employee with the right skill set. After all, skills can be taught; personality cannot.

Saje's story is just one of nearly two dozen other examples I'll share with you throughout this book, but more importantly, I want to come back to the point I made earlier. How you grow an organization's rev-enue and, in turn, its market share is less reliant on the technology and processes you adopt, and more about how you integrate and involve your people. That is the secret to becoming an unstoppable organization, some-thing we'll immerse ourselves into in the coming chapters. In this book, I'm going to share and show you new ways to market that are less about developing a perfect logo, and more about capitalizing on your people. I'll provide examples of companies that are selling differently than their com-petition, and capturing market share as a result.

What I've assimilated in this book are dozens of discussions and inter-views through my connections with CEOs, executives, and leaders from across North America who are at the helm of some of the fastest-growing organizations in the world. Their success comes down to carefully craft-ing a system and culture that supports closer connections between their employees and customers. Although the philosophy might seem simple, the complexity comes in building and evolving this connection. This is *not* an overnight event, but evolves through a series of specific interactions that both educate and involve employees in understanding the organization's vision, customer's needs, and how their performance, language, and interactions have a direct influence over each of these variables. In this book, it is my intention to shed light on how organizations such as Saje, Hillberg and Berk, CenterLine, and Blommer Chocolate, as well as dozens of others, have created sustained growth through building these connections. I will provide insights and ideas on how you can do the same for your organization, at little to no cost, by just changing the way you structure, approach, and lead your organization.

If this sounds like a trip worth taking, then grab a highlighter or note pad and buckle in because this will be a journey that will challenge how you think and, more importantly, how you act.

PART 1 WHAT IF EVERYTHING YOU KNEW ABOUT GROWTH WAS IRRELEVANT?

Referring back to my earlier point about so-called expert advice, there are predominantly two forms of advice that exist in the market today. The first suggests that CEOs, executives, and their teams should hunker down and focus on the "tried and true" methods that support growth such as brand building, customer acquisition strategies, and sales closing techniques. On the other hand, more and more information on the topic of revenue growth would suggest that all purchasing for products and services is moving online, hence the key to growth in today's market is to introduce the software and technology that supports a virtual marketplace. What I'd like you to consider, however, is what if this information was only partially true? In Part 1, we explore these two points of view and the specifics behind them, crafting a clear vision of today's customer, how they think, behave, and more importantly, what will make them take action and invest money.

1

SUCCESS OR FAILURE IN BUSINESS RELIES ON ONE THING

There is not much new under the sun.

Ray Casemore, Retired

When I was around the age of six, my parents took me to the local fair where, like any other kid my age, I took in the rides, various games, and demonstrations. The memory is long past today; however, the one thing that stands out in my mind was the magician who was demonstrating card tricks. I remember being amazed at the magician's ability to allow me to pick a card, without him actually seeing the card and then, after the deck was shuffled, to pick out the very card that I had chosen (or so it would seem). As a six-year-old living in a small town, I was absolutely astonished. Magic and specifically card tricks actually still amaze me to this day, as I spend time watching specials with magicians such as David Blaine[1] who, through sleight of hand, is able to amaze complete strangers with card tricks and other more dangerous feats. David, like many other magicians, is able to shift perceptions, making onlookers believe something that isn't real. The question I've asked myself during the past 10 years of research into what makes an organization unstoppable when it comes to growth is: are we being led to believe that the secret to growth isn't what we think it is?

For several years now, I have been traveling through North America and speaking at CEO and executive forums such as Vistage International and TEC Canada. In the hundreds of interactions I've had with CEOs, executives, and business owners, our discussions invariably turn to business growth. Sometimes it begins with some innocent small talk. I invariably ask, "How's business?" Other times, the questions come directly from the executive, who is seeking advice on what I've seen working that would help their organization grow. I was motivated to write this book as a result of these discussions. To be honest with you, I think the secrets to becoming an unstoppable organization aren't so secret. Instead, I believe that the real key to growth, the primary consideration necessary to truly becoming an unstoppable organization, has been somehow lost or forgotten amidst the glitz and glamour of new technology or lost as a result of chasing a solution that some guru might suggest is the "key to organizational growth today."

Now before I go any further, let me share with you that I've been an acting management consultant for more than a decade. I have never during this time believed or suggested I was a guru; rather, I'm a student of the hundreds of executives and organizations with which I've had the pleasure to work for. They have demonstrated time and time again through both their successes and challenges that, to grow a sustainable and profitable business in any sector and any region, you need only focus on one thing: people.

When I say people, what I'm referring to are your employees. They are the people who make decisions, interact with customers, and invest a good portion of their waking hours to the success of your organization. It's your people who will determine ultimately whether your organization is profitable or not, is successful or not, and will sustain it in a competitive marketplace or not. This might seem like an oversimplification; however, I can reassure you it's not. When you consider that every single person who works within your business today has a different background, experiences, ideas, expectations, and beliefs both personally and professionally, the objective of aligning your people in support of becoming an unstoppable organization can seem a daunting if not impossible task. In reality, it can be. However, it's for these very reasons that it's your people who ultimately are the deciding factor between the success and failure of your business. Your people are the key to becoming unstoppable.

Throughout this book, I'm going to demonstrate exactly why people who work in your organization today, and who may be working in it tomorrow, are the single most important factor to its future success. There can be no better area to invest your time, energy, and money than in your people. I'm not suggesting in making this statement, however, that you need to run out and train your people, nor do I believe that hiring more or better people is the answer. It's not as simple as that because as I alluded to, people are complex beings.

We have to think of our organizations as living, breathing entities that contain perceptions, norms, and ideals that ultimately influence the success or failure of the organization. These come from the people who work within it and the customers that it serves. It is our employees who determine the level of success (as measured by sales, productivity, profitability, and the like) an organization achieves, and it's the degree to which our employees feel committed to the success of the organization that will determine that success. Put differently, you can train employees on new processes, add new technology, or bring in highly skilled people, but in the end it's the employees' own experiences, ideals, and enthusiasm that will determine how well we attract, service, and retain our customers.

When my family moved to a new home last year, I contacted a local satellite provider to arrange for equipment and installation of our Internet and television. Everything went off without a hitch. About a month later, my wife and I decided we wanted to install a third satellite box to operate an additional television in our basement, so I contacted "customer support" about getting a third box. I was told that it would cost nearly $400, which seemed ludicrous considering that our existing dish and two boxes had only cost $225 just 30 days prior. As I felt my blood pressure rise, I explained to the customer service agent that the cost made no sense. I was reassured several times that this was the price.

As you might imagine, we decided not to add the third box, but instead to move our business to a different provider. A couple weeks after I cancelled my service, I received a call from my original provider to ask why I had made the move. When I explained the cost differential and our disappointment, they responded with, "Why sir, a third box should only have cost you $99 and being a new customer the agent you spoke with should have offered it for free." Those were my thoughts exactly, but unfortunately either the original agent didn't know this was the case (which could be for various reasons), or didn't care about the influence this policy may have had on my desire to keep them as my provider.

I'm sure you've had similar experiences, and I share this specific example because it highlights something that plagues most organizations today when it comes to becoming unstoppable. Employees of the organization, in their daily roles in supporting its objective, either don't know what to do or how it is to be done or, alternatively, they simply don't care. This statement isn't meant to be negative in any fashion; it's simply the truth. When it comes to acting in a way that best aligns with organizational objectives and satisfying customer needs, most employees either don't understand what specifically the organization wants or needs them to do, or they've realized that the role they are in or the organization they are with simply isn't for them.

Relative to employees not knowing what do to, the underlying issues can be:

- Not having sufficient or timely information to make decisions.
- Not having access to the tools to support making decisions.
- Not having the authority to make decisions.
- Not understanding the influence their decisions have on the business.
- Not being clear on the decisions others around them are making.

Relative to employees not caring about what they should be doing can result from:

- Not enjoying the work.
- Not enjoying the people they work with or for.
- Not having the support of leadership.

- Not believing the organization has their best interests at heart.
- Not believing they can make a difference in the business.

Whether an employee doesn't know or doesn't care can really depend on the situation at hand and the employee, but we can draw a hypothesis relative to causes when we consider the environment and challenges most companies face today.

Trials and Tribulations

My father once told me, "There is not much new under the sun." What he was referring to at the time was my concern as a young teenager about some bullies at my school who were taking names and picking fights. Like most bullies, they strutted their stuff through the halls of my high school, bumping into people, shooting looks at those they didn't like, and welcoming anyone to join them at the front of the school for an "attitude adjustment" after the final bell. Unfortunately for me, one of the more disliked hoodlums started dating my ex-girlfriend (yikes!), following which I presumed it was only a matter of time before I received an official invitation to the school parking lot for an attitude adjustment. As you can imagine, I was somewhat nervous. I shared the situation with my father, hypothetically of course, presenting a story about a guy who was being threatened by others at school, one of whom may have a knife, and asking what my father suggested my "friend" do if confronted. My father, who I'm sure got into a tussle or two when he was young, shared with me a story about guys carrying chains when he was younger, and suggested that the rumors were most likely not true and started by the bullies themselves as a scare tactic. Although I'm confident my father knew that my hypothetical story was about me, he ended our discussion by sharing this. "Shawn," he said, "there have always been bullies in schools and there will likely always be bullies. There is nothing new under the sun. Regardless of the difference in our age, there is nothing that you have or will face or experience that I or my father likely didn't experience ourselves."

If you're wondering, I was eventually invited for an "attitude adjustment" after the final bell, and following my father's sage advice I went and waited, somewhat nervously, to accept whatever fate was coming my way. After some exchange of words, the bully decided to save bruising his knuckles on my face for another day, which never came. What I've never forgotten, however, is my father's view that "there is nothing new under the sun." I find this piece of wisdom surrounding me daily, particularly when reading the news. Rarely is there a story or a situation that hasn't happened before. Each time we are faced with a record temperature high, the statement is followed with something like, "The last time we saw a high of this magnitude was back in 1951." When faced with the recession of 2008/9, the media, while reporting the severity of economic events happening globally, frequently referred back to the Great Depression of the 1930s. Sure, these situations and others like them might emerge in different forms or ways, but rarely is something completely new, never having been experienced before.

I share this story with you because that lesson my dad taught me comes to mind when considering the trials and tribulations of many organizations, and specifically, the CEOs and executives who lead them. Despite the growing complexity of a global marketplace, the continued evolution and influence of technology, and the challenges in adapting to shifts in human behavior and preferences, one thing remains constant. We have always been attempting to find ways to get the most from our people in order to best support our organization and its customers, and this likely will never change. At the core, an organization and its ability to be successful or not relies on its people—that, in essence, is my father's timeless wisdom at work. There is nothing new under the sun.

Consider, for example, that according to a survey of 1300 CEOs conducted by PwC, one of the top concerns globally for CEOs in 2017 is the challenge of "balancing man and machine."[2] That is, finding the right skills and technology that will allow them to marry technology with unique human capabilities. Furthermore, what's even more interesting about the survey responses is that a significant percent have found and continue to believe that technology has and will have a lesser effect on the growth and success of their companies than they once predicted back in 1998. What we can further glean from these insights is that regardless of the extent to which technology has and will continue to influence the growth of an organization, people and their unique talents and capabilities become ever more important. This isn't to say that continued developments in artificial intelligence and other technologies won't influence this perception in years to come, but it's important to note that when survey respondents were asked about their most pressing needs, finding and retaining talent were amongst the top three areas identified. More specifically, when asked about which specific skills were most important for them to find in the people they needed, the following five skills were identified:

- 61 percent said problem-solving was a crucial skill.
- 61 percent identified that adaptability was essential.
- 75 percent suggested leadership was necessary.
- 77 percent identified creativity and innovation.
- 64 percent selected emotional intelligence as a key skill.

The results of the survey highlight a few critical points about growing an organization in today's global economy, and they are in stark contrast to what many have believed in recent years, mostly on account of what "experts" have been suggesting. Specifically, despite the once strong belief that technology was going to change the face of business and people as we know it, this has not actually been the case. Although technology and its proper development and adaptation are crucial to remaining competitive, it has not and will not take the place of people as the most important resource for an organization seeking to grow and be profitable. Moreover, the more reliant we become on technology, the more we realize the importance of specific and unique human skills that can never be fully or effectively adopted by technology.

The question that logically presents itself, then, is how can we avoid becoming enamored with the latest and greatest technology, forgetting about the importance of our people? In my experience, the answer lies in what we have always known. A great organization, one that is successful and sustainable, is built on people. You might believe this isn't much of a revolutionary statement and that you are already placing your people first. However, to confirm the extent to which this might be true, let me share with you a simple exercise I use with my clients to assess the priority of their people relative to becoming an unstoppable organization.

Step 1: Add up the total investment you have made in technology during the last three years. Costs typically include researching, buying, and introducing technology (including training, annual registration costs, and so on). Add to this any ongoing costs you have for existing technology such as annual subscriptions, upgrades, and storage fees. Last, add all online costs, including Website development, maintenance, and so on. Any personnel costs associated with this technology should also be lumped into this bucket.

Step 2: Add up the total investment you have made in further developing the skills of your people. This typically comes from the training budgets set forth by each department and may include personal development for employees (for example, time management) or group development (for example, leadership training). Specifically, do not include development that is considered "supportive" versus "necessary." For instance, if you have compensated employees for furthering their education, but this education cannot or is not being applied on the job, then do not continue to pay for it.

For bonus material to assist you in your journey toward becoming an unstoppable organization, make sure to visit *www.unstoppable organization.com.*

When you compare these two costs, which is higher? In my experience, it's typically the former more so than the latter. The investments made to introduce and maintain technology far outweigh the investments made in developing people. If you want a simpler test to see this in action, pull up the invoice for your last ERP (enterprise resource planning) implementation and compare it to what you spent on the development of your leaders last year. I think you'll find a big gap in cost, with the lion's share of the investment having gone to the ERP project.

Although this is only a simple exercise, the investments we make in our people (and I'm not talking about wages, but rather how much we invest to strengthen their knowledge and abilities) are minor compared to many of the other expenses we have in operating a business. It's almost as if we see a wage as the primary motivator of our people, when we know this isn't true. In essence, I believe that we have our priorities wrong, and we are putting our proverbial wallets behind it and then often wondering why our organization, and specifically the people within it, aren't performing to the extent we'd like to see.

The Journey Is as Important as the Destination

I was reminded of just how widespread the perception that technology is the solution, rather than a tool, during a recent discussion with a former colleague. I was picking up my two boys from an after-school program one day when our paths crossed, and he felt obliged to give me an update of what had transpired since I left the company more than 10 years ago. What was interesting about the discussion was what this employee (a key contributor to his department) shared.

There had been a change in leadership, with the former vice president having left the department and a new one taking on the role. As a result of the new vice president coming on board, there were proposed "changes" in data reporting and metrics that were identified as necessary. Several of the senior managers (whom I had very good relationships with and significant respect for when we worked together) had clearly disagreed with the VP's ideas, having moved on to take jobs in other departments. As a result of the perceived changes in data and metrics, the new VP had determined that a change to the ERP system was necessary, with an initial price tag in the tens of millions of dollars. If you've ever been part of an ERP upgrade or installation, you know that the initial investment is usually the smallest investment made through the life span of the software, often only five years.

I asked my colleague what his thoughts were relative to these changes, and his response was one I hear all too often when senior employees are faced with a change in software after years of perfecting their processes in alignment with the previous software. "Let's just say that I'm looking at other options in my career," he stated. In other words, he was looking to get out. Now, what do you surmise the result will be of this department losing not only a respected and high performing VP, but also several key managers (with the potential for more senior people moving on), and being faced with introducing a new ERP platform that will more than likely change how every employee operates in their daily roles?

The reality is that introducing this new ERP platform will be a chaotic shift that will cost millions and millions of dollars and reap little to no improvements in performance, productivity, or morale. At the risk of being judged, don't think for a moment that I'm against technology because I'm not. Clearly, upgrades to technology are necessary in today's data driven world. But in this instance, where the decision to move to the new technology platform was made by someone in a senior role without including the input, feedback, or ideas of the primary user group or the leaders who oversee this group, the outcome becomes predictable. I know this from personal experience. Like you, I have been through numerous technology upgrades in my former corporate life, and each time I experienced the fallout of disgruntled employees, reduced productivity levels, and unrecognized objectives that were the drivers for the technology in the first place. Call me a doubting Thomas if you will, but any change to technology that is not driven by employees is a change that will be painful to introduce and nearly impossible to streamline. I'm not against technology; I'm against making decisions that do not include input and feedback from the primary drivers behind an organizations performance—its people.

Technology, although a tool, is meant to support a desired outcome, yet it's our people who will have to endure the journey. New technology is disruptive, and of course this disruption can yield benefits if done correctly. But where is the predominance of the investment in money and time typically spent when it comes to introducing technology? In my experience, it's not with the people.

Fundamentals to Success

Technology is obviously a significant contributor to continued growth and prosperity for organizations that want to compete in today's global world. In my first book, *Operational Empowerment*, I shared the example of Larsen and Shaw, a privately held company that specializes in the manufacturing of hinges, and their introduction of a simple chat feature on their Website as a means to capture leads from prospective and existing customers who visited their Website. This might seem like a simple idea. However, for a manufacturer focused on proven sales methodologies, having someone specifically manage the chat on a daily basis meant, at least initially, additional costs toward something that was unproven. Larsen and Shaw decided to make the leap, carefully selecting and working closely with the employee who they felt would be most comfortable with using the technology. Although not in a sales role at the time, the individual they selected was key to setting up the chat tool, developing scripts, and supporting the development of a chat-to-sales process. Although the chat module, a piece of software added to the company's Website, made broad claims about the ability to sell, the team at Larsen and Shaw knew that it would be by selecting the right employee, someone versed with the technology but also well connected within the organization itself, who could quickly respond to and satisfy customer needs. This was not a software first, employee second approach, but rather completed in unison with the employee being provided the autonomy and support necessary to build out the process.

If you are wondering how the transition went, the organization made its first sale to an online chat customer within six weeks of introducing the software. Unlike the example from my former colleague, this was an employee first approach to introducing technology, and the results speak volumes to its success.

Recognizing that people are primary to success is fundamental for an organization's growth and long-term prosperity. The degree to which your employees participate in or are responsible for the changes within an organization will ultimately determine the extent of its success. I recently shared this view with a CEO in the form of a golfing analogy. There are typically three different kinds of weather for golfers:

Good weather where there is little wind, and with the right level of skill it's not difficult to drop the ball onto the green where you plan to.

Challenging weather where wind directions and speeds make it more difficult to land the ball where you are intending.

Difficult weather where severe wind conditions make it next to impossible to hit the ball in the direction and distance you intend.

Employee responses to organizational change are similar to the wind. If employees understand and support a change, it's more likely the change will happen faster and more effectively than if the employees push back against it. Pushback requires more effort, time, and investment to improve adaption, and more often than not, the results will be "in the rough." In using this analogy, we can categorize employees and their willingness to accept or adapt to change into three categories:

1. Employees who are supportive and eager for change.
2. Employees who are neutral about a proposed change and can be convinced either way.
3. Employees who adamantly oppose a change.

The key, then, to building an unstoppable organization is to recognize that employees are primary to success over all else. The outcome of this as a fundamental philosophy shifts how an organization thinks, acts, and

FIG 1.1

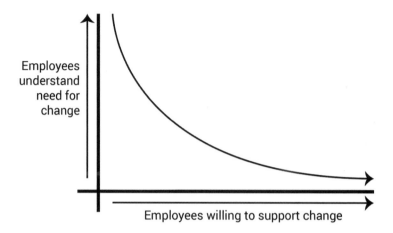

behaves. It influences the thoughts and actions of the board, the CEO, and senior and middle management. It breaks down the barriers in communication between frontline employees and those making the decisions that influence the organization. This, in turn, influences virtually every aspect of a business, including:

- How employees are hired.
- How leadership interacts with employees and teams.
- How communication flows both bottom-up and top-down.
- How employees are exposed to various aspects of the business.
- The connections built between employees and customers.

Lessons from Unstoppable Organizations

An unstoppable organization is one that puts its people first and recognizes that technology and various other resources are simply tools that should support its people in being more effective in their roles, rather than a crutch that replaces their roles.

2

WHAT WE BELIEVED TO BE TRUE ISN'T

The more you engage with customers, the clearer things become and the easier it is to determine what you should be doing.
John Russell, President, Harley Davidson

Recently, I reached out to a friend from decades ago named Paul. During our teenage years, Paul and I worked at the local grocery store stocking shelves and packing groceries. We reminisced about the fun we'd had, the bosses we survived, and some of the unique customers we had encountered during the nearly 10 years we spent working together. The job itself was fundamentally quite simple—pack groceries without damaging them, be courteous to customers, keep the store clean at all times, and of course, do anything else a supervisor or manager asked you to do. Back then, the store was in its early days and customers flocked in the doors, creating a literal mad-house at times where there was not even a shopping cart for incoming patrons to grab.

During my time working as a grocery clerk, I witnessed a steady decline in the number of patrons coming to the store. I didn't know it at the time, but there were some significant forces that were influencing this steady decline in business. Of course, because my paycheck wasn't directly influenced other than a slight reduction in my weekly hours, which was offset by small annual increases in pay, I wasn't too concerned. Neither were many of the other employees, for the very same reasons.

Fortunately, that grocery store is still alive in my hometown today. Notice I didn't say, "alive and well"? The last few times that I've stopped by, I've been stunned by the lack of customers. There is often only a handful throughout the entire store, which begs the question: "How can they afford to keep the doors open?"

Having stayed in touch with several of my former colleagues from those days, including the former general manager, I've heard various perspectives on why the store began its sharp decline in sales more than 20 years ago, and why it continues today. Warning: despite these being isolated to a grocery retailer, my guess is that some of the following statements might sound familiar to you.

Former managers believe that the continued decline in investment in the store made by the head office, in conjunction with the steady increase in pay and benefits for the employees, is the underlying issue that has ultimately led to the store's current unhealthy state.

Past employees believe that the unwillingness of management to listen to and act on their ideas to update the store layout, making it more appealing and welcoming to today's customers, has resulted in the decline.

The few *remaining employees* who still work at the store are desperately praying for it to remain open until they can retire, often citing the local economy and increased competition of new grocery stores as the primary reasons for the store's decline.

The reality is that *all of these conditions* have actually led to the store's current state. As sales have declined, the grocery chain has invested less money in marketing and reduced its investment in many of its stores, choosing instead to redirect any revenue to stores in more largely populated areas that were financially thriving. Competition that has grown in both brick-and-mortar stores with newer layouts, better features such as in-store restaurants and coffee, combined with growing competition online for grocery customers, has also further exacerbated the decline in customers and revenue. Continued increases in overhead to operate the store, including employee wages and benefits, are obviously hard to swallow when revenue is on the decline, which only serves to further diminish the availability of cash to invest. Add to this that employees who have remained working in the store and who remember "How things used to be," are often the very first to suggest, "We tried that before—it didn't work" when it comes to introducing new ideas. This resistance makes improving the current situation even more difficult.

I share this example with you not to focus on the grocery industry or this store in particular, but to demonstrate that the growth challenges facing many organizations today are all too common regardless of your sector, region, or tenure in the marketplace. When you look behind the walls of many organizations, you'll find they are struggling to grow (or even survive!) for many of the same reasons I just outlined. Sure, this doesn't apply to all organizations, as there are a choice few who have grown sporadically, and others who have increased their revenue and market share through acquisition. But we can predominantly place most organizations on a bell curve to identify their success at achieving profitable growth. In the following figure, I outline how using a bell curve can clarify how elusive sustained and profitable growth can be.

FIG 2.1

In this chapter, I'm going to take on the notion that growth in a business is achieved only by those who figure out the magic formula of combining great marketing campaigns with strong selling processes underlined by a product or service that keeps customers coming back. In fact, in my experience, it's these very notions that have led to the continued decline in both sales and revenue of many organizations today; often, it's the result of listening to and following the same advice and practices that have been around for decades.

We'll discuss how, despite all of the noise around the complexity of today's customer, in fact, they are simple to understand, reach, and influence. In addition, we will dispel the myth around business growth that suggests "more is better," and that doing more of what you've always done, just faster and better, will ultimately lead to winning more sales and closing more business. Lastly, I'll introduce the concept of employee intelligence as a business growth tool; a strategy that underlies all of your efforts to achieve sustained growth; how it works, and the value it brings.

So let's tackle the age-old question. With limited funds and time available in a competitive and changing marketplace, just what exactly is an executive or entrepreneur to do in order to put their business on a sustained growth trajectory?

The Simplicity of Today's Customer

To answer the question of where to invest time and money to achieve growth, we need to first step back and assess the needs, both emotionally and logically, of today's customer and consider if and how they have shifted. To begin, let's first consider a question that I often use when helping CEOs and executives set their strategic vision:

"How have your customers' buying preferences changed?"

Before you read any further, you might wonder, why would we look back rather than forward? Why not simply jump to drawing conclusions about our future customer needs, rather than reflecting back on what's done, particularly when we all know that customer needs have evolved? The answer is simple. By considering the past, we can inform the future. As Winston Churchill once said, "The farther back you can look, the farther forward you are likely to see."[1]

You might also wonder why we would look back several decades when your business may have only been around for a few years. The answer is quite simple and hinges on our discussions from Chapter 1: people are the primary consideration when it comes to becoming an unstoppable organization. Organizations are built upon the knowledge and ideas of the people who work within them and, therefore, are shaped based on the extent to which its employees are permitted to share their experiences and ideas while practicing and applying their talent.

A friend of mine recently changed careers after a 10-year career as a regional marketing director at a well-known international chain. During her time with her former employer, she led a team of people heading up the organization's customer-facing campaigns, including their in-store marketing campaigns. She was well known and respected for her ability to connect and collaborate with operators of branches in ensuring marketing campaigns were accepted, adopted, and successful. She had very little experience with or exposure to using technology. Lured away by an opportunity with a new and growing organization, and seeking a change after several changes in management, she is now in a new role leading a team to develop an online strategy for attracting customers, a stark contrast to her previous role where much of her interactions were face-to-face and in-person. Her new employer, knowing her background, has decided to have her lead the development and execution of their online strategy, knowing full well that her marketing experience is heavily weighted on in-person and in-store marketing. This might seem like a miscalculation or mistake on the organizations part; however, it's quite ingenious. They recognize that our past experiences influence our perspectives on how we move forward, and that my friend's experiences in dealing historically with customers in a face-to-face environment will actually be beneficial when developing and executing an online strategy. Having gotten to know customers in a personalized fashion during the last decade will ultimately ensure the success of the online investment.

In building out her strategy, I spent some time with my friend to assist her in making connections between the world with which she is familiar and the one she isn't. We reflected back upon those areas that have historical significance when it comes to understanding our customers, their needs, and behaviors. I share these areas as a means for you to reflect on your own organization and the history of your customers. Whether your organization is still in its infancy or quite mature, considering the history and evolution of people as individuals is a relevant exercise to help ascertain where the organization needs to focus moving forward.

As a starting point, take out a piece of paper and consider the following areas as it pertains to your customers and the changes in how they think, act, and behave.

Generational differences: What are the typical ages of your customers, and specifically, what are the distinctions in how each generation behaves? Consider that Baby Boomers are much more comfortable making purchases in person or over the phone, whereas Millennials predominately prefer and are more comfortable with making purchases online. By identifying the distinctions in each of the generations that make up your customers, you can bring significant clarity to what has and continues to change relative to your customers' needs and expectations.

Decision-making preferences: How are your customers making decisions today as compared to a decade ago? Customers today research everything online and through various social media platforms prior to drawing a conclusion. Research often includes entering search words or key phrases into search engines such as Google (this has become so engrained in society that "Google it" has become an acceptable phrase in the English language—look it up!), as well as asking friends and acquaintances on various social media channels about their experiences and feedback. In effect, decisions today rely much more heavily on *untrusted sources* than on a close group of friends or past relationships.

Communication preferences: The preferences in how we receive and send communications have changed significantly. In this consideration, venture beyond simply looking at the preferences of each generation and consider geographical region, the availability of technology, and the influence of social and economic factors. Consider that print advertising and communications are much less prominent in some parts of the world. Last, consider the influences that technology has had on the three primary means of communicating—namely, visual, audio, and kinesthetic.

Attention span: What is the average attention span of your customers today as compared to a decade ago? How have any changes in this area influenced their ability to connect with your marketing campaigns, tolerate your customer service response times, or find relevance and satisfaction in your product or service? If you haven't already found it, you might want to check out the study conducted by Microsoft where they measured and compared the average attention span of people back in 2000 at 12 seconds, and doing the same test in 2013, only to find that attention spans had diminished to eight seconds—one second less than a goldfish.

Community: Another consideration I have my clients reflect upon when identifying changes to their customers is the influence of community. Consider that in the early 1990s there were few cell phones in use by the general public and the Internet was in its infancy. People who were physically present around them were the ones influencing customers, including their family, friends, neighbors, and coworkers; ideas on what to purchase and who to buy it from were based on this close-knit community. Today, our community is different. It's not uncommon to have several hundred friends on Facebook (a community that you custom build based on the friends you connect with and the pages you like), most of whom you may never have even met. The decisions we make today on what to purchase and who to buy from are mostly based on this much larger community of weaker relationships, and as a result, our buying decisions are more broadly influenced.

What you will find by working through this exercise is that there have been and continue to be significant changes that influence how and what your customers buy, the products they prefer, and the brands they support. The fundamental needs of customers haven't changed (remember, there is nothing new under the sun), which is an indirect outcome of this exercise. Our customers still purchase goods, they may just wish to purchase them in different ways; they still make decisions, but differently than they once did; they are still influenced by the thoughts and opinions of others, but where and how they solicit these opinions has evolved into larger communities, which include online communities rather than just the community in which they live or physically participate.

By completing this one simple exercise, you now have the foundation for what is necessary to begin to build a plan of growth for your organization. It's by reflecting on the changes in people that you have now clarified what you may be doing or not doing that is (or isn't) influencing your customers' decisions to test and purchase your products or services. The needs of today's customers are actually the very same needs of customers from several decades ago, which are closely connected to the needs that were outlined in Maslow's hierarchy of needs back in 1943.[2] What *has* changed, however, is how customers seek out, assess, and decide upon how their needs will be satisfied.

Why Doing More Doesn't Grow Revenue

Last year, I was hired by a distribution company to give a kick-off talk to their sales and marketing team. When I met with the CEO, who had started the business some 30 years ago, to discuss his perspective on the organization's challenges and determine how we might best position and structure the talk for maximum effectiveness, it became clear what the underlying problem was. Sales and revenue had been relatively flat for several years, and as a result, the CEO and his executive team had brought on new product lines in an effort to boost sales. Selling more products to existing customers seemed like a good idea. Unfortunately, however, sales of the newly introduced product lines had been minimal, while sales of the existing longstanding products were continuing to decline. The CEO was in a panic.

I had a sense initially about what the problem might be. However, I set about interviewing several of the sales, marketing, and customer service staff to obtain their ideas and feedback. My hunch was validated.

The company had never completed the exercise I shared with you earlier of looking at the changes in their customer base through the past several years. Rather than address the underlying issues surrounding their decline in revenue (for example, relevance of products, evolving buying practices, shifting customer needs, and modified decision-making influences), they instead took what appeared to be the easiest route to growth by increasing the size of their offerings. Surely if customers didn't want to buy existing products, they might be interested in other products?

The CEO and his senior executive team made a few critical errors in this situation, which I set about to correct. First, they never consulted with the employees who were facing customers to discuss and assess ideas on how to overcome the declining sales (their reasoning was that they feared it may spook their employees into leaving the company). Second, they listened to a sales "expert" who suggested they already had customers with existing relationships; therefore, their best approach was to offer new products. Third, they decided to take this approach because they saw it as the quickest solution to overcoming their problem.

I see this kind of "throw it at the wall to see what sticks" strategy being deployed all the time. Employees are sheltered from the issues for fear of scaring the good ones away. In turn, someone in the executive team makes a decision with very little counsel to take the fastest and least disruptive route possible while giving little consideration to history or how they might have gotten to their current state in the first place. This is the power of letting history inform the future. When we reflect on these shifts in influences on what makes customers buy, most organizations have decidedly tried to do more, which in many cases only serves to further diminish focus and efforts to achieving growth. Ultimately, the idea that "more products equal more revenue" is a false perception, and often results in more equaling less.

The idea of adding new product lines to drive more revenue and offer more products to existing customers might make sense in theory, but it often fails to be effective for three key reasons:

1. Customer buying preferences aren't clearly understood, resulting in a larger disconnect between customer needs and the value that your employees provide.
2. New product lines grow the size and complexity of both your catalog and your operation, but are often introduced and managed using the same number of staff that managed the smaller catalog of offerings.
3. Employees engaged in the marketing, selling, and delivery of such additional services are forced to shift from intimately understanding their products and customers to becoming a clearing house for a plethora of items that no longer hold relevance or priority in their mind.

You may notice a theme among these three points. If we consider our earlier discussion on how customer buying and decision-making preferences have changed, it becomes obvious that today's customers having greater demands about their own personalized needs. You needn't look any further to see this in action than your local grocery store. Look at the variety of products that exist on the shelves. Where there were once two types of Coca-Cola products—Coke and Diet Coke—there are now these products as well as Coke Light, Coke Zero, Cherry Coke, Coke with Lime, Caffeine Free Coke, Coke Life, and on and on. In order to satisfy growing customer preferences for individualized and specialized products, the biggest brands have resorted to providing more and more options. However, additional products do not typically result in higher profit. My uncle, a long-time fan of Diet Coke, now prefers the taste of Coke Zero. As a result, his investment in Diet Coke has been redirected, but has not resulted in Coke selling more products. True, creating a new product that is in direct competition with a competitor's product makes sense, but the expansive product lines that many companies are introducing are no longer serving the purpose of opening up a new market; rather, they are catering to individual customer preferences at the risk of losing them. Using my uncle as an example, it's the "suggested" additional health benefits to drinking Coke Zero that lured him away from Diet Coke, not a competitor's product.

This is a key realization when it comes to growing revenue because more products create greater complexity in an organization. It means, for example, that those working in sales are responsible for pitching more products (which means they need to be intimately knowledgeable with more products). Manufacturing has to produce more product lines, resulting in more raw materials, more WIP (work in progress) inventory, more changes in product processes, more training for staff, and so on. Adding more products and features is at the core of the "throw it at the wall to see what sticks" strategy. Yet in doing so, we often detract from the very essence of what makes a customer buy in the first place, and indirectly doing so often creates greater complexity in an organization, which makes it more difficult to be good at what we do.

Based on our discussion above, then, how can an employee create and sustain a personalized interaction when they are consistently dealing with new customers, more products, and greater complexity amongst the depth of those products? The reality is "more" only results in less:

More products to market often result in employees focusing on a volume of activities rather than targeted campaigns that hone in on customer value.

More products available to sales personnel reduce time available in the sales process for understanding and personalization, and instead, shift the sales processes toward a demonstration of product volume.

More products that require production create a higher margin of error for production staff in managing a broader catalog of products, all with their own unique production processes and instructions, thereby diminishing quality.

More products for distribution often results in increased error rates in shipping, greater shipping costs (for example, expediting to account for shipping errors or delays), and a lower fill rate per transaction. When faced with this type of environment, most employees simply resort to what they believe their only option to be—push volume.

The ability to successfully grow a business of any size and in any sector requires consideration of the customers who purchase the product or service, but just as importantly, a consideration of the people who support its success. Taking an approach toward growth by focusing on adding more products, more features, or more services results in employees often resorting to the "throw it against the wall to see what sticks" approach, which diminishes the customer's overall experience.

If you're looking for a simple test to confirm whether your employees are stuck in this approach, try the following:

1. Ask a small group of customers for their preferences relative to ensuring the best possible buying experience. Incorporate questions that determine how clear they are on what products you currently offer; how responsive and personalized your company's approach to selling is; satisfaction with the receipt and application of the product itself; and the ease of access to your employees in the event of questions or issues with the product.

2. Using the same questions, speak with employees in various parts of your business to determine their perceptions on your customer's responses. In essence, uncover how aligned your employees are with the feedback from your customers.

3. Lastly, assess the gaps between responses to determine where the greatest issues might lie. For example, are sellers focused more heavily on pitching products than they are in understanding customer needs? Are employees providing a personalized experience when faced with customer inquiries?

For bonus questions and other supportive materials, make sure to visit *www.unstoppableorganization.com.*

Just as our customer's buying preferences have changed, so too has the world around us. In essence, it might seem like offering more products is the best approach to capturing more sales and more revenue, until we understand the influences this approach has on directly satisfying customer needs through our employees. So if more products and services aren't the best approach to creating sustained organic growth, you might start to wonder if focusing on fewer products or services is the better choice. It's not.

Blending Old With New: Why Traditional Approaches Alone Won't Work

During the past several years of consulting with organizations on how to become unstoppable, I'm often faced with pushback on introducing new methods of growth. In my experience, many CEOs and executives have achieved success in their organization by predominantly focusing on a single successful method, be it a high quality or unique product or service; a strong brand promise supported by effective marketing campaigns; proven effective selling strategies and tactics; or highly responsive and knowledgeable customer service. It's not uncommon to find a couple of these at play at the heart of a successful company, but I've yet to find the existence of strength in all of these areas. What this means is important because it influences the organization and its leadership. Where a company has had success that can be tied back to a specific approach that was used in the past, the leader of the organization and often much of the management team falls prey to frozen thinking. This type of thinking limits the ability to see new solutions and creative ideas that can yield new and different results—often necessary as customer needs and demands have changed, resulting in a slow diminishment of customers, sales, and revenue.

If having strong in-print marketing campaigns yielded the most leads during the early years of the business, then it is often believed that continuing these types of campaigns are the cure for diminishing revenue.

If a proven sales process once produced the largest quantity of new business, then it is often believed that any loss of customers or revenue is the result of the process not being effectively followed or applied.

If a responsive and knowledgeable team of customer service representatives were what customers in the early days of the business raved about, then any diminishing revenue must be tied directly to poor customer service.

In every instance of this frozen thinking, it is employees who are often considered the primary point of blame for not "following the process" or "for taking matters into their own hands." As you can imagine, once this perception reaches employees, their morale diminishes, which only serves to further exacerbate the problem.

Just because something worked once doesn't mean it will continue to be as effective. Remember, the purpose of history is to inform the future, not create it. That's the lesson, and breaking through frozen thinking is the first obstacle to opening up the possibilities for what needs to change in order to meet shifting customer needs and demands. After all, it's rare that I've come across a CEO or executive who doesn't think their customers have changed, yet they and their teams are often still relying on practices or approaches that were effective in the past rather than exploring what might be working in the future.

Traditional approaches are not completely ineffective, nor are they wrong. What's important to recognize is that as with the preferences of our customers evolving, influenced by a variety of social, economic, and technological factors, so too do our approaches to growing an organization need to change. Just because something worked once doesn't mean it will automatically work again; in fact, it is highly unlikely that it will work if applied in the same method again. Here are some examples I'm sure you can relate to:

Marketing strictly through print ads or only online will yield fewer leads than marketing through a combination of the two strategies.

Selling using face-to-face strategies, or only through using online methods, will be far less superior to generating and closing business than a combination of the two approaches.

Manufacturing goods while following lean practices, without considering technology, Six Sigma, or a variety of other proven production improvement methodologies will yield lower throughput and diminished productivity.

The key is to blend approaches, and the way to determine what of the old needs to remain versus what of the new should be created or introduced comes from assessing your customer. If the demographics of your customers has shifted and more of your buyers are using the Internet to shop, adding a shopping cart and possibly supportive chat functions on your Website makes sense. However, keeping traditional selling methods that were historically effective with older generations is also crucial to sustaining your business.

One of the best examples I can give you of recognizing the effectiveness of blending the new with the old is cold calling. Once an effective means of finding leads, cold calling is now considered dead by many. This is true if you apply cold calling in its historically acceptable application. The advent of technology, such as caller ID, has made it more difficult to get people to pick up a phone, never mind generational differences in customers who are often more hesitant to answer the phone today anyway. If you blend a historically effective selling strategy such as cold calling with newer technology, and contrast it against customer buying preferences, new and more effective strategies emerge which can help warm up the cold call and ensure a higher response rate.

For example:

- Calling to follow up on an e-mail inquiry submitted online.
- Calling to follow up with customers who purchased a product online.
- Calling to follow up based on an e-mail introduction from a referral source.
- Calling as a follow up to an e-mail sent at an earlier time.

For years now, some of the most iconic brands have been applying this blended approach. Nike and Apple blend their historically strong retail presence with strategic sales channel partners, complemented by an online presence allowing their customers a multitude of options when it comes to seeking out and purchasing products.

The need to blend the old with the new comes not only as a result of changes in our customer buying and behavioral preferences, but also as a result of these very influences impacting our employees. Although these influences might manifest themselves in different ways when it comes to our employees, understanding their influence is key to assessing how to effectively blend traditional approaches with more modernly accepted ways to grow an organization.

Employee Intelligence: The Unknown Secret to Growth

It's one thing to recognize that our customer buying preferences have evolved and changed, but it's another to recognize that many of these changes have also been adopted by or influenced our employees. As a result, attempting to direct employees in marketing, sales, or customer service to use practices that no longer work or seem irrelevant can be further detrimental for growth.

While delivering a speech to a group of CEOs on empowering customers, I asked the audience what methods of customer communication they found were most challenging. One CEO of a privately held business spoke up quickly and said, "Shawn, this texting thing with customers, it is absolutely outrageous." At first, I took his statement as a positive response, so I asked him to continue. It turns out that by "outrageous," what he meant was "ineffective." When I asked him to elaborate, he shared that many of his sales personnel liked texting their customers. It turns out that in one instance a customer had misunderstood a text message, and had taken their business elsewhere. As a result, the CEO had instituted a policy of no texting allowed.

That's right, as a result of one misunderstood text (out of literally thousands) not only did the CEO decide by himself to limit texting with customers, but he applied a blanket policy across the organization to completely ban texting with customers. Surprised at his response (as were several others in the room, confirmed through their chuckles and whispers), I asked how the policy was holding up. "Not well," he proclaimed, "it seems the only person following the policy is me, and none of my managers want to police it."

I don't care what kind of business you have; texting, chat, or instant messaging is here to stay. If your customers prefer to communicate in that manner, you'd better find a way to make it happen unless you prefer to lose them. Here is what I said to the CEO: one bad customer experience should never equate a change in policy, particularly if that policy limits or detracts from how your employees interact with or support your customers. Once you use policy to institute a change, you detract from your employees' ability to think and act responsibly and with common sense.

I don't recall what the exact issue was with the text message that irritated the customer, but the CEO's response was unwarranted. It's unrealistic to believe that an accepted form of communication that both your customers and employees feel comfortable using should be restricted on account of one person's poor judgment or misinterpretation.

Herein lies another secret that every unstoppable organization has realized. Policy and procedures, although meant to drive consistent behavior and results while avoiding repeatable problems, limit creativity and slowly erode employee morale and engagement. Think about that for a moment; an abundance of policy and procedure is actually an obstacle to growing a business and its revenue because it turns employees into robots. The more we tell people what to do, the less they have to think. This results in employees who wander through the days acting like robots. I'm not saying this to insult the employees, but you and I both know that growth of an organization, built on attracting new customers and keeping existing ones, comes from your employees' ability to satisfy the individual needs of customers.

If you agree that our customers' needs and demands are changing, then our employees, who are also influenced by the same environmental factors, are also changing. As a result, tapping into the intelligence of our employees, such as their knowledge of how customers prefer to communicate, their understanding of the shifting needs and demands of customers, their insight into the weaknesses within our products, services, or customer interactions, provides the ideas, information, and opportunities to build a stronger and more collaborative interaction with our customers. I like to think of employees as an organization's secret weapon to growth. How you apply that weapon is the key to long-term success.

Lessons from Unstoppable Organizations

Unstoppable organizations recognize that growth does not come as a result of applying past practices for increasing sales and revenue because today's customers and employees are different. Growth comes as a result of focusing on unlocking the potential of our employees, while serving our customers in means that they prefer.

3

"CUSTOMERIZATION": THE AMAZON EFFECT

*If you do build a great experience, customers tell each
other about that. Word of mouth is very powerful.*
Jeff Bezos, CEO, Amazon

How Can You Adapt to a Growing Need for Customization?

Earlier, I introduced you to Kate Ross LeBlanc and Jean-Pierre LeBlanc, the founders of Saje Natural Wellness. Amidst their ambitious plans for growth, there were four areas Kate and Jean Pierre focused on as fundamental objectives of their strategy.

1. Create a consistently outrageous customer experience. When it comes to their customers' experience, an "outrageous customer experience" isn't just a slogan for Saje. In every retail store, team members greet you as you enter, invest time in

getting to know you as an individual, provide natural wellness education, as well as make recommendations about which Saje products will best support your wellness and improve your life. What's recognizable is that Saje team members truly want and are empowered to connect with community members and share the health benefits of using natural products. The focus is on providing incredible natural wellness education, not on making a sale. As Kate says, "Seeds that are planted don't have to be harvested in a day." Team members are empowered and encouraged to practice "outrageous" customer service. Regardless of whether the investment a customer makes is $5 or $50, how they are treated remains unchanged.

2. Build a community around the Saje brand. Kate and Jean-Pierre recognized early on that to build a strong and loyal following, they needed to cultivate a community of like-minded people. Building a community began with sharing their passion of natural wellness with the world through efficacious products offered in environments centered on education, hosting wellness experiences and seminars, and nurturing a growing digital community. Saje has captured the minds and hearts of their community members, making their brand a one-stop center for all things wellness.

3. Stand 100 percent behind the quality of your products. A product is only as valuable as the guarantee behind it. This is where Saje stands out amongst other retailers. Customer service is not something they provide; it's part of who they are. Kate and Jean-Pierre have built a culture of empowerment over fear; team members can make decisions based on what's best for the community member, and what would be considered "outrageous." One way this shows up is in their return process. Community members can bring a product back if it's not serving their wellness to replace it with something that will. In addition to customer service, product efficacy and a commitment to 100 percent natural ingredients is their other founding pillar, and something they passionately stand behind.

4. Empower team members to service customers' needs. As we discussed in Chapter 2, with the increasing demands of customers, Kate and Jean-Pierre recognized that there was only one method of ensuring a consistent customer service experience, and that was championed through their team members. Whether you're on the retail floor or a member of the CX (customer experience) team who answer phone calls, e-mails, and live chats, team members are empowered to make decisions that they feel support the company's customer service pillar. Customer service guidelines are clear yet broad in scope, allowing team members freedom and autonomy which lay the groundwork for exceptional experiences and interactions with the brand. As a result, Saje lacks the restrictions and restraints that most company policies contain. To continue serving their community as it grew, Kate and Jean-Pierre realized that attracting the right, like-minded team members, nurturing their talents, and providing them with the freedom to make decisions were the keys to their long-term success and directly related to the scalability of outrageous customer service.

In speaking with Kate (and as proven through the significant growth of Saje), these founding pillars provide the cornerstone for Saje's continued expansion plans. Although some of these fundamental elements might sound familiar to other organizational objectives you've heard in the past, the difference is in how the Saje team is completely and emphatically committed to living and breathing them. After working with Saje team members and speaking with Kate at length, it becomes readily apparent that the secret to Saje's success is not so much a secret as it is common sense (and you know what they say about common sense—it isn't always that common). Saje has achieved significant and sustained growth on account of becoming clear on and supporting objectives that are necessary to satisfy the growing needs and expectations of customers today. They recognize as owners and as an organization that having a dominant retail presence is only possible if their retail was supported by a strong online presence and community of customers. In turn, a strong online presence and community would only be successful if supported by an expansive retail presence. Growth for an organization today requires considering historically accepted practices (in this instance brick and mortar retail) in collaboration with new methods for satisfying customer needs, such as providing an online shopping experience that is complementary to the retail experience. One is not built or led in isolation of the other, but rather built and supported in unison as a way of providing an almost 360 degree shopping experience for their customers, both existing and potential. The drivers behind this collaboration of in-store and online retail includes:

Customers have virtually unlimited options when it comes to searching for and selecting products and services. Whatever is most convenient for them at the time is when the customer decides to shop.

Customers are highly influenced by online information, which can be accessed within seconds. Having an online community of information allows existing and potential customers a quick and easy means to access information and educate themselves on the benefits of wellness and the products Saje carries to support a better lifestyle.

Customers' buying decisions are influenced through social proof that is broader in scope and nature. By building a community amongst their customers, Saje draws upon the natural compliments and outspoken benefits its customers are pleased to share, allowing the organization to obtain social proof for would-be customers who are considering making a purchase from Saje. This unsolicited social proof is the referral source of the 21st century.

Consider the last time you made a buying decision, and I'll bet nine times out of 10 you did some research online. Booking travel plans likely included reviewing online what others had to say about the hotel or resort you considered staying at; purchasing a car included reviewing the price of the car, as well as online reports through sources such as consumer reports to determine the quality and durability of the car; eating at a new restaurant began with first checking out their menu and customer reviews on Websites such as Opentable.com or Zagot.com. Sustained growth of an organization cannot be achieved without considering how customers' demands and needs can be best satisfied, which today is about building a community of followers who share your organization's passion for its products or services. Saje is passionate about wellness and by creating both an online and in-store experience for its customers, allows existing and would-be customers who are passionate about wellness to share in the Saje experience.

When I share this type of information during a speech, it's not unusual for a handful of the CEOs or executives in the audience to approach me after the talk and say something like, "But Shawn, we aren't a retail business, so we can't be online," or, "This might make sense for someone selling direct to a consumer, Shawn, but we sell direct to other businesses, so this online stuff doesn't make sense."

I'm the first to admit that a retail-facing business requires more activity when it comes to being present online to connect with and nurture customers and prospects, but even in a business-to-business environment you are still dealing with people. That's the common theme that most who are in a business-to-business environment and who downplay the role of blending both in-person and online experiences have, but I'll tell you what I tell them. If you truly believe that having a solid online presence, supported by employees who are empowered to satisfy your customers needs, is only something that is relevant for a retail business, you are dead wrong.

Let me share something I presented in my first book, *Operational Empowerment: Collaborate, Innovate, and Engage to Beat the Competition* to prove this point. A client of mine from many years ago, Larsen and Shaw, are known as "The Hinge People." In fact, they have been manufacturing hinges for commercial and residential application since 1919. Although predominantly supporting customers in a business-to-business environment, Mary Jane and the team at Larsen and Shaw realized that the considerable traffic they were experiencing on their Website was in fact an opportunity to connect with both existing and potential customers. This was despite not having any specific products for sale on their Website, only displays and product drawings. The question, then, is why wouldn't Larsen and Shaw try to connect with some of the visitors to their Website through a chat module? Fast forward about 90 days later, and Larsen and Shaw had not only introduced the chat module on their Website, they had also aligned someone comfortable with the technology to engage in dialogue with visitors to their site, and had closed several sales as a result.

This simple example demonstrates my point that even in the business-to-business (B2B) marketplace, customers are still people and social media and various other online technologies are necessary to engage with customers. The lines between what a retail business focuses on to engage with customers and what a manufacturing or wholesale business engages in have blurred. Today, the online chat tool that Larsen and Shaw has is used in conjunction with other standard selling practices, allowing for engagement with prospective customers and defining and nurturing their needs before moving to e-mail, telephone, or in-person communication.

But it's not just the addition of a chat module or an online customer acquisition tool that yields these new selling opportunities. It is the result of introducing the right employees, those who are versed in and comfortable with engaging in discussions online, possessing the knowledge of the company's products and sales methodologies, who make this approach a success. When I spoke with Mary Jane Bushell, the president of Larsen and Shaw, she said that the growth of online selling for this predominantly B2B manufacturer has relied not only on technology, but also on having the right people who are willing and able to take ownership of and become empowered in selling in this new environment.

When we reflect on these examples from two very different organizations, one selling direct to consumers and the other selling direct to businesses, and both with a track record for sustained growth, a few things become clear as necessary components for growing an organization today:

1. Customer centricity is a business objective that is crucial for long-term success.
2. Multiple communication channels are necessary to satisfy broad customer preferences.
3. The lines between selling retail and selling to business are blurring as technology evolves recognizing that, in both instances, the sale is still to a person.
4. Empowering employees is a key strategy that is necessary to satisfying the needs of today's customers.
5. Employee fit within a role and within an organization is primary to employee skills, which can be taught and learned.

To see these strategies in action in a more recognizable organization, we need look no further than the behemoth of Amazon, one of the most recognizable organizations in the world today.

The Amazon Influence

We've discussed how customer needs and demands have evolved, and it's important to recognize that many of these demands have been through learned behaviors, driven by the growing ability of organizations to be and offer more to their customers. If Domino's Pizza, for example, hadn't created a brand promise that offered pizza "in 30 minutes or it's free," then it's possible that the expectation we have that all pizza should arrive in 30 minutes would never have been adopted and expected. If banks would never have extended their hours to include evenings and Saturdays, we would still be willing to wait patiently in long line-ups at the bank between 9 a.m. and 4 p.m., Monday through Friday. If automotive manufacturers had never extended their warranties beyond three years or 60,000 miles, we would likely be accepting a lower standard of quality and longevity in the cars we drive. You get the picture. In order to stand out from the competition, virtually every organization attempts to set itself apart by creating a unique promise to its customers. If successfully achieved, this promise often becomes the customer's "new expected norm" as far as their expectations go. In today's' retail shopping environment, we need look no further than Amazon to see this in action.

If you've ever purchased something on Amazon (and AC BloomReach Inc. found that more than 55 percent of people go to Amazon first when searching for products[1]), then you've likely become accustomed to the convenience and affordability they provide. You've likely also become accustomed to the convenience of one-click shopping, a feature whose technology was proprietary to Amazon. However, other online retailers such as Apple and Barnes & Noble are now also incorporating one-click buying for their online customers. As the popularity of one-click buying has grown, so too has demand for software that can achieve similar magic. Companies such as Stripe have built such software and are now offering it to the broader marketplace as a tool that can be incorporated into a Website or online shopping cart.[2] What was once a unique and proprietary benefit of shopping on Amazon is slowly evolving into a more broadly adopted and in-demand feature that, in turn, will influence online shoppers' expectations for single-click buying features for all of their online needs.

McDonald's has also recently introduced select-and-pay kiosks in many locations, offering customers the choice of individualized or personalized service. From a restaurant point of view this may seem new, but when you consider that many banks have a teller standing by in addition to a bank machine, the concept becomes another example of something that was once unique influencing customer buying preferences. When I met with an executive from McDonald's following a talk I gave on generational differences, he said that this transition to kiosks reduced the necessity for having multiple employees behind the counter taking orders. Initially doubtful that this was anything more than a ploy to reduce the number of employees that McDonald's had at each location, the executive said it was quite the contrary. What they realized in speaking with customers is that although the food was served quickly, there was little support in the seating area for customers who needed help. By introducing technology where orders were being taken, it provided customers the choice as to how they wanted to place their order (which satisfied a growing customer desire), but also allowed McDonald's the option of redirecting employees into the seating area, another growing customer need. In both instances, this move helped to further set McDonald's apart from their competition. This is a great example of making shifts in the organization that serve the changing desires of customers, while furthering the organization's competitive advantage.

How did the likes of Amazon and McDonald's come up with these unique features that set them apart from their competition? Here are some questions you can use with your team to uncover these opportunities for your organization:

1. What changes, improvements, or new features are your customers seeking that they can't seem to find in a similar product or service to yours?

2. What are other industries or sectors (that serve the same customers, but with a different product or service) doing to satisfy the needs or desires of their customers? How might you incorporate similar practices? (Think about parallels such

as how a drive-thru that works for fast food also works for banking customers.)

3. What is your competition not doing that you could do to further serve the needs of your customers? How could you make your customers' experience even better than it is today?

4. What shifts can you predict will occur in the next five to 10 years in how your customers seek out or purchase your products or services? What might you do to introduce new features or options into your organization that will satisfy these shifts?

For bonus materials, make sure you visit *www.unstoppable organization.com*.

In my experience, despite the impact of the Amazon influence on customer needs and expectations, most organizations are missing out on a tremendous opportunity to build a brand promise that even their greatest competition cannot challenge.

Customerizing: What it Means and Why You Need to Do It

When Jeff Sziklai originally purchased a little packaging company in a small town, they had wildly ambitious goals. The challenges that stood in their way were enormous, particularly for a small packaging company in a rural location. As the organization grew, Jeff never let go of one thing. The success of the organization would ultimately rely on the success of the people who worked for and supported it. From the early days of taking over the business, Jeff and his team set about creating a strong culture with a family atmosphere. When Jeff would arrive at work each day, he'd take a moment to walk the floor, saying good morning to everyone. He and his team introduced profit-sharing as a way to build employee ownership in the business and its future success. And every few months Jeff would walk out onto the production floor and speak with the employees, discussing challenges with customers new and old, changes in competition, and pressures and influences in the marketplace.

In the early stages of the business, Jeff knew that in order to compete, the company had to stand apart from their competition, both large and small. They needed to create "the Amazon effect" with their existing and future customers so as not to succumb to the ever-growing pressure from their competition. It became clear early on that in order to best satisfy their customers' needs, Jeff and his team needed to dramatically reduce the lead-time for their product, something that their competition was unable and, in many instances, unwilling to do.

Through their efforts, and as momentum grew within the culture, Jeff and his team were slowly able to chip away at the time it took to build their product, often turning around small orders in only days, when it took their competition several weeks. As word spread about what this little manufacturing plant was achieving, more customers became interested in how they might serve a specific niche where small volumes and rapid turnover were needed.

Jeff and his team built a business (now with eight facilities around North America) on understanding and satisfying their customers' needs in a way their competition couldn't. They achieved this with and through their employees, who took pride of ownership in the roles and in the organization as a whole, helping to satisfy a customer niche in the market that has allowed the organization to flourish for well over 20 years now. Of course, their continued improvements have been complemented by investments in new equipment and technology, but as Jeff suggests, "As our company has grown, it has been critical to ensure that the culture and vision of employees and customers (in that order) continues. As we increase our management team, it's critical that each manager must promote the culture that we worked so hard to create."

An unstoppable organization is one that remains in tune with what their customers' needs and desires are for both today and tomorrow. They empower their employees, placing them at the forefront of supporting and creating a unique promise that will in turn satisfy the evolution of customer demands. Your customers want customization, and it's through your employees that you can actually define and meet this growing need.

I have helped dozens of organizations create and fulfill their unique customer promise by focusing first and foremost on their people. Although often completed through a series of collaborative discussions, I will share with you the process we take so that you can do the same within your organization.

Step One: Assess Your Current Ability to Satisfy Customer Demands

1. What is your unique brand promise that lets you stand apart from your competition?
2. What are all the ways you deliver this brand promise today?
3. How successful would your customers say you are at meeting this brand promise?
4. How do your employees support your brand promise?
5. What changes or improvements could your employees make that would elevate the consistent value of this promise?

At this point, you should have enough information to identify *how* you can further improve your brand promise. The solutions cannot be introduced or improved in isolation, but instead require a commitment from your people in order to be successful. Put differently, your ideas are just that—your ideas. To ensure your plan for improving your customer experience is sound and successful, you need input and buy-in from your people. As a result, the next step in achieving your unique brand promise is to introduce it to your employees for their feedback and ideas. Step two in this process is as follows.

Step Two: Employee Input

1. What do your employees believe is your unique brand promise (UBP)?
2. What ways do they believe exist today to deliver that UBP? Where are you strong as an organization? Where are you weak?
3. What changes should be made to further improve the delivery of the UBP?
4. What do they need in order to satisfy these changes?

Following step two, you will now have enough information to build out a plan to further clarify and improve your UBP. Information is only one part of the equation and is effective only if your people are engaged in actually delivering on your UBP.

Preparing Your Employees to Customerize

Engaging your employees in the process I just outlined is not a one-time initiative, but a long-term commitment. Jeff and his team have been working on building and delivering a consistently unique experience for their customers for nearly two decades now because as each day passes, customer expectations continue to grow. Where Jeff's team was once able to turn around a small order in a matter of days, his team must now do so in less than 48 hours because as time would have it, their competition's ability to turn around orders has also lessened. With this continuous pressure to identify and make improvements, you might think the road to becoming an unstoppable organization is unachievable. Fortunately, this is not the case, though it demonstrates that being unstoppable through the long-term requires a long-term commitment. As they say, Rome wasn't built in a day.

Satisfying shifting customer demands is something I like to call "customerization." It's important to recognize that there are some fundamental shifts necessary that are counter-intuitive to much of what we have come to know as organizational norms. Employees who are in a position of thinking and acting in a way that satisfies growing customer needs require a different way of thinking about their roles within the organization. Rather than start by describing what the environment is like for employees in companies like Jeff's, however, I want to start by describing the environment for what it is not.

Employees in a customerized environment are not:

1. Stifled by an abundance of policy or process that directs their every move or reaction.
2. Limited in their ability to respond to customer demands.
3. Required to escalate every customer issue or concern that falls outside of existing norms to leadership.
4. Powerless to respond to customer needs when time is of the essence.
5. Isolated in their interactions with one another in an effort to "maximize productivity."

Before I continue, take a long, hard look at these descriptions. Do any of them describe the working environment within your organization? If so, don't panic. It is not unusual that at least two of these descriptors align with the culture and environment of an organization, though more than three means you've got some significant work to do.

You may wonder why I started with what a customerized environment is not, rather than what it is. Well, in my research from nearly 100 organizations globally, those that have mastered an environment that consistently satisfies growing customer demands have a foundation that is built upon a different philosophy than what we are accustomed to. Consider that in the Industrial Age, which took its origins from the military, structure, process, policy, and respect for authority ruled. There was little consideration for the individual differences of customers (Henry Ford made the Model A in any color a customer wanted, as long as it was black) or employees for that matter. Obviously, in the post-industrial era, we have become more in tune with what our customers and employees need. In my experience, the foundation that the company was built upon typically still relies heavily on what we know "used to be true."

When Aviva Leebow Wolmer, CEO of Pacesetter Steel, took over for her father, she entered an industry that was built in the industrial era—steel. Historically, organizations in the steel industry, where the environment consisted of extreme conditions on account of the processes necessary for manufacturing steel, were operated on the premise that people were resources necessary to operate equipment. Aviva, having grown up in the industry, knew that in order to survive in today's marketplace where talented and committed employees are often just as hard to find as great customers, she must set out to change the face of Pacesetter Steel. The results have demonstrated she is on the right path.

Aviva and her team created an environment where employees are encouraged to collaborate with one another, while leadership shifted away from the historically accepted command and control model to one of facilitating dialogue amongst employees. The entire environment hinges heavily on constant and open dialogue in the form of daily meetings and coaching sessions that occur in relaxed environments. It's through these constant communications that Aviva and her team are able to stay at the forefront of ensuring customer needs are understood and proactively acted upon. Customerizing is the foundation for Aviva and the team at Pacesetter Steel.

As with Jeff and his team at Bellwyck Packaging, Aviva suggests there is no stopping the evolution of her team. As vision boards display employee ideas, recognition, and outstanding achievements both within the organization as well as with customers, Aviva strives to create an environment in which employees have the desire, motivation, and most importantly, the ability to consistently improve their customer's experience.

Shifting from a culture of set policies and procedures in serving customers to one that allows for customerization requires a shift in how employees think and act as it pertains to their customer interactions. There are five steps you need to perform in order to prepare employees for this transition:

1. Hold frequent dialogue with employees, ensuring information flows both top-down and bottom-up.
2. Create environments that facilitate communications amongst employees, removing barriers such as walls and cubicles.
3. Shift decision-making from frontline leaders to employees.
4. Create boundaries instead of policies. Let employees know limitations in decisions and actions rather than specifics.
5. Create collaborative hubs, building team knowledge through sharing ideas and customer interactions.

With a clear understanding of the distinctions and practices that set unstoppable organizations apart, let's shift gears a bit and discuss how the realities in today's marketplace are influencing these unstoppable organizations in preparing for tomorrow.

Lessons from Unstoppable Organizations

An unstoppable organization is one that provides customers with a customizable experience that is, in turn, supported and delivered by employees who have the freedom, knowledge, and desire to provide such an experience, recognizing as they do so why it's important.

PART 2 EXPLORING THE REALITIES OF TODAY'S MARKETPLACE

Much of the evolution of the needs and demands of today's customers have been influenced by the advancement of technology. It's not so much the technology itself that has influenced customer expectations, but rather the growing access to real-time information which has influenced customer decision-making, buying preferences, and quality and service expectations. Just as today's customers have evolved, the employees have too. With greater access to information, a growing desire to blend their personal and professional life, and increasing comfort with instability, today's employees might seem to only further exacerbate the complexity of the working environment. When you consider these significant changes that have occurred in the people who both work in and buy from our organization, it doesn't take long to realize that our approaches to marketing, selling, and servicing customers have fallen behind. Similarly, our understanding of what employees need in order to remain productive and committed has not progressed.

In Part 2, we explore what specifically has changed about our employees who are working in our business, producing products, delivering services, and interacting with our customers through marketing, selling, and customer service. More importantly, we discuss how we can capitalize on the evolution of our employees to better serve and satisfy our customers, building an unstoppable organization from the inside out.

4

VALUE IS IN THE EYE OF THE BEHOLDER

If people believe they share values with a
company, they will stay loyal to the brand.
Howard Shultz, Chairman, Starbucks

It goes without saying that in order to achieve steady and predictable growth in sales, revenue and profits for an organization results from consistently delivering value into the marketplace. The challenge, however, is that each customer tends to define value differently. In Chapter 3, we discussed addressing how to influence the perceived value of a product or service through customerization as I like to call it. Although it's true that the ability to offer customized solutions to customers to satisfy individual desires and needs has become a significant driver in building customer awareness and (ultimately) investment, it isn't the only consideration.

To determine the perceived value that a product or service can have, we can learn a considerable amount from understanding what successful organizations, those that appear to be virtually unstoppable, do in order to sell their products into a highly competitive marketplace at above average prices. Reflecting on this for a moment, what companies tend to come to mind? I immediately think of Starbucks, selling coffee at a premium that is typically well above that of their competition, while dominating their space in the market. Whether you are a regular patron of Starbucks, or are astounded at their prices and refuse to buy their product, there is no one that I've come across who isn't aware of the Starbucks brand. The question we must ask ourselves is why does a segment of the global market prefer a cup of coffee from Starbucks when they can simply buy a coffee machine for their home, making a similar cup of coffee within minutes in less time than they would likely spend in the lineup and at a fraction of the price? (You can even buy Starbucks coffee in various forms for use with different coffee brewers.)

This question has been analyzed and debated for years with theories on why consumers continue to patronize Starbucks despite the lack of logic behind their decisions. Some have argued that Starbucks does a great job at marketing (and they do); whereas others have suggested that it's all about Starbucks unique ability of becoming part of their customer's habitual routines. Most of the ideas that have surfaced make sense, but when you study Starbucks and Howard Schultz's[1] take on the business, the most important aspect of why Starbucks has been so successful has been the result of its ability to create a unique and valuable experience for its customers through its employees. Think, for example, about the last time you entered a Starbucks and you'll recall a few distinctions that set its employees apart from other coffee or fast food retailers.

- Greeters are always friendly and quick to process your order (they recognize that any wait you've had while standing in line can be overcome with fast, courteous, and prompt service).
- Servers ask for your first name and handwrite it on your cup (each transaction is personalized from your initial point of contact with an employee until the point when the server calls out your name).

- Chatter and interactions amongst staff (which are in the open) are fun and friendly. It's rare to see employees behind the counter at a Starbucks not having a good time.
- Smiles are part of the equation. Employees treat customers with the same friendly, warm, and cheerful greeting each and every time, with smiles and a warm welcome despite the varying attitudes of their customers.

When you consider how a company like Starbucks has been able to create these environments amongst their locations globally, two things become apparent. First, these nuances are a key to Starbucks creating a warm and inviting atmosphere for its clientele; they add significant value in a market segment that is typically more focused on the speed of transactions versus creating an efficient yet inviting atmosphere. Second, Starbucks has created a culture of "customer first." It is intentional, and it breeds from more than just customer-focused training or great pay and benefits (the default ideas that many leaders have when considering how they might build a strong customer-centric environment). There's something much deeper and more complex at play.

What Starbucks has done is recognize that customers will actually pay more and remain loyal if their perception of the value of their experience equates to the investment they are making. Starbucks realizes that in order to charge up to double what their competition is charging for a similar product (coffee), they have to provide an experience that is more valuable to the end customer than their competition does.

Some of Starbucks' competition, organizations such as McDonald's for example, have built their reputation and appeal for their customers based on the realization that to attract and maintain their ideal customer in an uber-competitive fast food market (which in some instances includes competing with Starbucks!), they must consistently ensure a quick, convenient, and error-free experience where customers can place and receive their orders. McDonald's consistently satisfies this pursuit by training all employees on providing an exceptional customer experience, in conjunction with providing a wide variety of options for their customers, allowing them to pick and choose not only what is ordered but how it's ordered. For example, you'll recall I mentioned in the last chapter a reference to

McDonald's adding self-serving kiosks allowing customers another option in addition to a personalized ordering experience with someone behind the counter. Although the kiosk itself allows McDonald's to reduce the number of people serving customers behind the counter, in recognizing their competition (like Starbucks) is having significant success in creating a strong customer following by focusing on a positive experience, McDonald's is retraining and deploying their employees into the dining areas of their restaurants. For an organization to satisfy evolving customer desires and needs, the focus on adding value is a never-ending pursuit and one that hinges on the employees' ability to both understand and consistently deliver what customers value.

We can also look at Harley Davidson, which has recognized that in order to sell motorcycles for significantly higher prices than the closest competitors, the overall customer experience when entering a store, regardless of its location around the world, must equate in the customer's mind to the value of the investment made. It is rare to find anything cheap in a Harley Davidson store (I was recently told by a friend that HD actually stands for "Hundred Dollars," which is what I seem to spend every time I enter a store!). Similar to McDonald's, Harley offers a branded product (produced by others, but with ensured high quality and branded as Harley Davidson demonstrating such), providing value by ensuring their customers can customize their experience with a set number of available options. When I bought a Harley Davidson Street Glide a year ago, I was amazed at all of the ways in which I could customize the bike to my liking, from the exhaust to the handlebars and seat. The options are literally endless, which Harley has recognized and capitalized on, hinged on well-trained and educated staff that is always friendly and willing to service customers. Harley Davidson lives and breathes "customerization" with all of its products, and does so by ensuring its employees understand what customers value, and more importantly, how their customers can add value.

In each of these examples, it's the combination of a perception of customization in conjunction with the customer's experience with the product or service that demonstrates value. The question that remains after reflecting on these examples is how exactly do these companies assess, identify, and deliver value for their customers?

Providing Value: Why You'll Need Glasses

Inevitably, when I bring up conglomerates like McDonald's or Starbucks, most of the CEOs or executives I meet have a difficult time relating. With the longevity of each of these global brands, the global footprint they possess, and the resulting cash they pump out day in and day out, it's difficult to relate to or even contemplate exactly how to mimic their success. What I often suggest is that rather than consider the companies in their current state, consider how they came to be and the journey they took that ultimately brought them to their current level of success. I recently watched the movie *The Founder*, where Michael Keaton played the role of Ray Croc, the founder of the McDonald's Corporation and the person responsible for building the McDonald's franchise.[2] In the movie, the story depicts Croc as a traveling salesman who stumbles across two men who had developed a system for producing high quality food consistently and quickly during a time when restaurants and drive-thrus weren't fast and orders were consistently incorrect. Early on, the movie depicts the McDonald brothers spending literally hours with their employees, training them, and running through routines that mimicked the cooking and serving environments, all while having some laughs and fun in the process. The model the brothers created, and more importantly, how they involved their employees in understanding and adopting that model, was ultimately the key to their initial success and remains a standard for fast food production and serving today. The originators of this concept, Richard and Maurice McDonald[3], identified, honed, and tested their theory with their employees, building not only a level of commitment to the process for the employees, but also ensuring buy-in to the process by involving employees early on, before they were ever in the restaurant itself. Employees were clear on what they were there to achieve, and more importantly, how their specific role added value to their customers.

There are some deep lessons that can be taken from this approach the McDonald brothers took, most notably:

1. Creating a competitive advantage begins with understanding what your customers' true needs are, recognizing what they value, and knowing how that value can be delivered.

2. Moving from concept to realization in an organization requires a combination of process and people, initially defined and then honed and improved.

3. Commitment to the customer is achieved when employees participate in and take ownership in the process they use. Being told strictly what to do, with no context for why, has little staying power.

4. Providing a value-first approach to customers requires involving leadership in the process, working side by side and hand in hand with their teams.

5. Selection of team members with a focus on building camaraderie is the key to building a consistently valuable product or service.

You might be wondering why we don't see more organizations with the explosive growth and staying power of these global brands. After all, building a team of employees who clearly understand what customers value, and how their role contributes to providing this value, seems like a simple task, right? If only it were that simple. Before we answer this question, let's first be clear about something. Value has an extremely broad definition, and every person values something different. This creates a problem in understanding what your customers might value because it varies by customer and is based on their personal preferences and circumstances. For example, what I value in a restaurant can differ depending on a variety of factors. If I'm in a rush, then I place greater value on speed and quality of the order than I might on taste. If I'm taking my wife out for dinner, I place greater value on the environment and experience than I do on speed of the order.

To put it mildly, defining value for your customers can seem quite difficult, but you need to find ways to remain in direct contact with them to ascertain the range of value they place on the service or product you provide. For example, refer back to my point earlier in this chapter. Who in your organization interacts with your customers both directly and indirectly? Your employees do, of course. What would happen if you were to provide them with a brief script of questions that would allow both you and your people to maintain a pulse on feedback from customers by consistently asking a brief series of questions, collecting that feedback, and responding with changes or improvements? Not only will value become more apparent to your employees, but also any changes in response to evolving value for your customers may be timelier!

Let me share an example of how this can work and break down a simple approach you can use to understand what your customers value. A few years ago, I spent some time with an organization helping them to assess and define what their customers value. The process involved several customer interviews and focus groups. Armed with this information, I then worked with teams from across the organization to help them understand and connect with:

1. What influence they had, both real and perceived, on providing value to the customer.
2. How they might further increase their value on a consistent basis and the influences this would have on the customer, the organization, and their role.
3. What changes they could make in the organization that would influence the value of both existing and potential customers.

For a downloadable PDF of this exercise, make sure you visit *www .unstoppableorganization.com* to complete this exercise with your customers.

To demonstrate how we did this, here is an example. In the instance above, the organization had an accounting department that consisted of an accounts receivable clerk and an accounts payable clerk. When we began discussing how their roles added value to their customers, they were unable to provide any definitive answers. However, as we explored the different ways they interacted with the customer, value opportunities began to surface. The accounts receivable clerk consistently contacted customers who were past due on their accounts by e-mail. The clerk, upon recognizing that this interaction was an opportunity to understand what customers valued, realized that phone calls followed up by e-mails were likely a more powerful way to connect. In addition, she identified three questions that were key to consistently defining value in the eyes of these customers who, although past due on their accounts, were generally still good, longstanding clients. The questions were contained in a script as follows.

Initial Script:

"Hello Mrs. Customer, I wanted to give you a call as I recently noticed invoice 123 was 60 days past due. I wasn't sure if you were aware, but for your convenience we not only accept check, but we can also a accept credit card if that's more convenient for you."

Second Script (following first, regardless of response):

"While I have you on the phone, I was hoping to ask how your experience was with our product/service. Was it everything you expected it to be?"

If yes: "Great, I was curious, would you be willing to provide me with a brief testimonial based on your experience with the product/service?"

If no: "I'm sorry to hear that, how can I help?"

To provide you with some further context behind this script, the company struggled with outstanding accounts, but had never offered alternate sources for payment other than checks. In a day and age where credit cards and (more recently) EFT transactions have become the norm, offering alternate payment options only made sense. Upon introduction, the initial script and response from customers led to more than 40 percent reduction in outstanding payments beyond 30 days.

In regards to the second script, we considered the call and subsequent e-mail a customer touch point, meaning that we had an opportunity to create a personalized interaction with a customer. If done correctly, we could learn more about how valuable, or not, the organization's product/service was.

When you consider that virtually every employee in your organization today interacts with customers both directly and indirectly, the idea of assessing and adding value becomes much more realistic. This is the very realization that organizations such as Starbucks, McDonald's, and Harley Davidson had from the start. Every interaction has the opportunity to add value, if only for the employee's recognition and ability to do so.

Once you realize the opportunities that exist throughout your organization to add value to your customers, the minimal cost to do so, and the significant influence this approach can have, a flood of ideas and opportunities will come to light. However, this is not the ultimate benefit of integrating your employees as part of the value equation. It's in the competitive advantage this approach provides, building strong employee-customer connections that yield higher levels of customer loyalty, thus allowing you the opportunity to charge a premium for your product or service.

I realize this might seem like a tall order considering all we've done is helped employees connect their roles with adding value to your customers. However, when you consider that the higher value your customers receive (the measure of "higher" being value that exceeds what customers experience with your competition) equates to an ability for your organization to charge higher prices, then the real benefit of this approach starts to take effect. Take a moment to return to the examples earlier in the chapter. Starbucks charges more for coffee than their most direct competition, as does Harley Davidson and McDonald's. Higher value equates to higher prices, and that is the return that supports the consistent growth of revenue for an unstoppable organization.

To understand how to specifically assess what it is your customers value today, you need to consider the five aspects of value, which we will do in the next section.

The Five Aspects of Value for Today's Customers

As we've discussed thus far, your customer invests their money and resources based on a product or service, creating for them a perception that it satisfies their desired need. Needs vary by customer, and so do values. What someone values today in the purchase of a new car may be very different in a few years when his or her life circumstances have changed. What a customer values today in clothing may be very different in a few weeks when they learn of a move to a different climate or experience a change in their body weight.

To simplify the complexity of value, we need to consider the five aspects of customer value, the degree to which and priority of such varies with each customer and each individual transaction. What's important to mention is that these aspects can and have changed through time as a result of our evolution. Our value on "time," for example, is considerably different in today's generation than it was 20 years ago, as is the value we place on price.

The following are the five key areas in which today's customers assess value.

Social Proof

The continued emergence and growth in popularity of social media and the Internet has resulted in a broader willingness to use social proof and acceptance. Where a decision to buy a car was once solely based on your relationship with a dealer and the feedback from a few close friends, today that same decision can be influenced by what your 200-plus friends (some of whom you've never met or haven't seen in person in years) on Facebook have to say; the feedback from a few blogs of car fanatics who post reviews; and reviews posted on sites such as Google and Bing that tell you what others, often complete strangers, have to say about the car or the dealership.

Ease of Use

As time has become more of a perceivable scarce resource for North Americans, the need and desire for products and services that are simple to use, further simplify our lives, and in essence "give back time," has become in greater demand. Apple is a company that has built a reputation (and a global brand) on the concept that simplicity and convenience are the cornerstones of their products. In reality, with more apps consuming more time, this might not be the case. Regardless, simplicity and ease of use is something that customers today seek out.

Responsiveness

When Dave Carroll wrote the song "United Breaks Guitars" back in 2008, it was out of sheer frustration with the lack of response and support he received from United when they damaged his guitar during a flight.[4] United's response, unfortunately, came after the damage to their reputation was already done (the YouTube video Dave created now has more than 14 million views). Responsiveness also creates a sense of importance for customers of today, who have a greater expectation for customization to satisfy personal preferences.

Life Integration

With a greater demand for customization and more value placed on simplicity and time, the customers of today want products that help them integrate their life. Notice I didn't say "make their life better"? Integration is seen as a way to further reduce complexity and make life and all of its challenges and obstacles easier. Apple comes to mind as a company that has focused on the integration of its products; automobiles today are equipped with various apps to allow drivers to carry on conversations on their phones, hands free; and grocery stores have integrated a broader array of products, including clothing and pharmaceuticals in an effort to create a "one-stop-shop" experience for customers. The more effectively a product or service integrates for a customer, the more value they place on it.

Technological Intrigue

Now I'll admit that this may not seem as obvious as the previous aspects of value, but when you consider the pace at which technology has evolved, more and more people are willing to pay for technology (some are even obsessed with it). I'd suggest that autonomous cars, although still not fully integrated, will drive interest (pardon the pun) more because of the curiosity the general public has on how the technology works, than on the idea of a car driving itself. The benefits are huge, but how the technology works and being "the first to try it" has greater influence on value today than ever before.

You will have noticed that I left out the most historically recognized value contributors such as price or quality, and there's a reason for this. These factors, which were once highly valued by customers, and to some degree still are, have become expected norms. That is, we expect quality to be acceptable as part of the product or service, and we expect the price to be competitive. If they are not, we revert to using avenues such as social proof to determine if the price or quality is realistic. We only need to reflect back on our discussion of Harley Davidson as an example of this. Not only are Harleys expensive, but so are their parts! Trust me on this. When deciding to add a backrest to bring my wife along on trips, I quickly realized that just a backrest alone would be shy of $300 (hopefully she isn't reading this). When I asked others about the expense, they validated that yes it was expensive and yes that was the price, but as a Harley Davidson owner, you pay for the quality you receive (in other words, whining about the price of components and parts amongst a community of Harley owners will fall on deaf ears!). Social proof and life integration determined that the expense was justified!

Understanding how customers today assess value is critical for success as an unstoppable organization. But here we need to return to our earlier point of employees as the key to create, deliver, and offer value. Employees can influence each one of these areas, from social proof to technological intrigue. To do so we need to recognize that employees are in fact a conduit to delivering value.

Employees: The Value Conduit

As customers have become more informed and prolific in their desire to gain feedback through other sources prior to making decisions, they have also evolved in how they define what value is when it comes to making an investment. Increasing sensitivity to what a brand and an organization represent, product or service origins and benefits, as well as social influence have added to the already existent criteria of price, quality, and availability. As the definition of value continues to evolve, it might seem that meeting a customer's needs is almost impossible. If you are thinking this might actually be the case for your organization, then you'd be wrong. In every organization, there is what I call the "value conduit," a connection that exists between employees of the organization and their customers, both directly and indirectly, that ultimately influence the customers' perception of whether they are receiving value or not. Most importantly, the value conduit can override the actual value obtained from a product or service *regardless* of the quality, price, or availability of the product (historically accepted measurable means of value). This further supports the influence of more modern attributes of value that we discussed earlier, such as brand representation and social influence.

The value conduit is your employees, and the phases of the conduit are outlined in the following figure.

The five stages of value that a customer will progress through are influenced directly and indirectly by employees. Your employees have the single-handed ability to make or break a customer's perception of the value your company provides. The stages are outlined as follows:

Stage 1: Image. This is the stage at which customers perceive your product/service from a distance, such as when they hear things about your

FIG 4.1

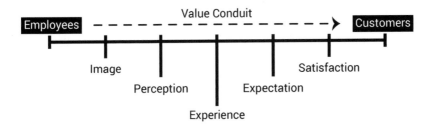

company, its employees, brand, products, community involvement, and so on. During the image stage, customers assess impressions of the value of your organization and its products or services, and determine whether further consideration makes sense. If it does, they transition to stage 2.

Stage 2: Perception. This is the stage at which customers begin to research and observe your organization and its products and services. This might include listening to stories from their friends or coworkers on their experiences, or checking out customer feedback online or through social media. If they like what they see, they next transition to stage 3.

Stage 3: Experience. Once the customer decides to try your product or service, they will make initial contact. Based on this contact, the customer will assess their initial experience to determine the extent to which it aligns with their perceptions.

Stage 4: Expectation. If the customer is satisfied with their initial experience, they will invest in your product or service (to varying degrees, depending on the strength of response in the previous stages and the extent to which their need will be met) and will immediately determine if the experience satisfies their expectations.

Stage 5: Satisfaction. If the customer's expectations have been met, they will continue to invest in your organization's products or services, and will do so as long as the experience satisfies their initial expectations.

Quite often in considering these stages, CEOs, executives, and leaders consider stage 5 as the point at which they need to engage their people, ensuring that expectations are continually met. As you can see, this is only one-fifth of the entire equation and we are bringing employees in too late to ensure they understand what customers value, and more importantly, how they can deliver this value. Let me share with you an example.

About two years ago we were considering moving our Internet and television service to a new provider. The organization had been around for decades and appeared (through advertisements) to offer premium services that aligned with our needs (stage 1). With this initial idea in our minds, my wife and I began to ask others who used the same provider about their experiences. We also began paying closer attention to the flyers that frequented our doorstep (stage 2). Eventually, we decided to contact the provider to inquire about specific pricing and services for our situation, engaging in an online chat (stage 3). The experience of the online chat seemed to align with our perceptions, and as a result, I called the provider to inquire about purchasing their services. This is where the wagon began to chart off-course. The final price on the phone was slightly higher than the quoted price online, and the agent who took my call didn't seem concerned with determining why this was or matching the price (this is a weak entry into stage 4). My wife and I, somewhat skeptical, decided to proceed with the investment as we had waited long enough, and arranged an installation of the service provider's equipment at our home. The installation went as expected, although the installer seemed to be having a bad day, grunting when we asked a question and leaving scraps of wire and remnants of connectors everywhere he went. At this point, having been through similar experiences with other providers, we accepted the weaknesses as an "industry-wide" issue, rather than isolated to this specific company. Our expectations therefore were met, though not entirely. At this point, we were now on high alert (never entering stage 5).

A few weeks later, we decided to purchase another controller in order to install a second television, and I called the company again. I was shocked to learn that my initial pricing had been considered "promotional," and as a result, any further equipment purchases were about three times my initial cost. Frustrated, I pleaded my case to the agent on the phone. They didn't seem the slight bit concerned. After speaking to my wife, I called the agent back and cancelled the service, deciding instead to move to our second option for a service provider.

I share this example not only to demonstrate the phases, but also to point out something that might not be so obvious. Regardless of your product or service, one thing stands commonly between all five of these stages of the value conduit: your employees. At each and every level, customers, both existing and potential, are assessing your products or services with and through your employees, be they in sales, customer service, production, or otherwise. A poor quality product that is produced at a manufacturing facility will influence your customer's perception of quality, and is indirectly influenced by your employees—some might argue it's directly influenced.

My point is simple. Organizations that are unstoppable recognize the influence their people have on the value customers perceive and receive of their products and services. The question, then, isn't whether your employees influence your customer's perceptions of value, but to what degrees and in what ways. Once you define this, you are at a significant competitive advantage to position your people to escalate and sustain high levels of value that your customers simply aren't getting anywhere else.

Lessons from Unstoppable Organizations

Today's customers assess the value they will and are receiving from products or services based on the experience they have with an organization's employees. Helping employees understand and act as a conduit to customer value will further increase the value customers receive.

5

THE INFORMATION HIGHWAY OR ROUTE 66?

Knowledge is power. Information is power. The
secreting or hoarding of knowledge or information may
be an act of tyranny camouflaged as humility.
Robin Morgan, American Poet, Author

Seeds for Growth

When you consider the complexity created by the rapidly evolving needs of today's customers and employees, it's no wonder that organizations struggle with achieving significant and sustained growth. As one CEO put it during a meeting in which we were discussing some these challenges, "Shawn, if I'm not dealing with a customer issue, then I'm dealing with an employee issue. There seems to be little opportunity to actually focus on anything else with all these people issues we're dealing with." People issues indeed. But when you stop to consider for a moment what is at the heart of these challenges, it doesn't take too long to realize that information, or access to information, is a significant driver behind many of the changes organizations are experiencing. Of course, it's technology that is influencing much of our ability to access information, the speed at which we can access it, and ultimately providing a means to make more personalized decisions around the information and our interpretation of it. As a frequent flyer, for example, I use an app called Flight Tracker.[1] The app provides me with real-time information and status of flights, most of which is often more accurate than the information I can obtain from employees working in customer service at the airports. With this information in hand, I no longer need to spend hours waiting in a long line at the customer service counter when a flight is delayed, but rather, I can make alternate travel plans that minimize the impact on my schedule. This access to information maximizes the use of my time and gives me the "inside information" once possessed only by the customer service agents at the airport. When an announcement is made that a flight is delayed, I often know more than those who don't have the app in hand, and I'm in a position to know exactly what a "slight delay" means, rather than guessing as to what the service agent considers as "slight."

As Claude Shannon says, "Information is the resolution of uncertainty."[2] Although most organizations are placing a tremendous focus on providing more information to their customers, consideration also has to be made for what and how information is shared with employees. After all, as we first discussed in Chapter 4, it's employees who are interacting with customers both directly and indirectly on a daily, if not hourly, basis. When I mention this during my talks on how to build an unstoppable organization, invariably I'm told that with all of the e-mail, texting, instant messaging, company intranets, and the like, employees today have access to far more information than ever before. This, of course is true. However, the problem is that much of this information rarely provides the employees with exactly what they need to make more informed decisions on the job and specific to serving customers. Don't get me wrong, communicating information to employees is always a good thing, but the power comes when you are clear about what information you're sharing, why it's important, and specifically what employees can do with the information that will better satisfy your customers. Telling employees about changes in the organization's share price or updates to the benefits program is fine, but what we have to ask ourselves is exactly how does this information help the employee make better decisions on the job? The short answer is it doesn't.

In my work with some of the fastest growing organizations in North America, it has become readily apparent to me that unstoppable organizations and the executives and leaders who run them have made this connection in providing information strategically to their employees. Such leaders often see their organization not as employees and customers in isolation of one another, but rather as a collaboration of sorts in the form of a melting pot for growth. The more executives invest in their people, the greater the results they achieve from a business perspective.

I briefly mentioned Aviva Leebow Wolmer, CEO of Pacesetter Steel (or Team Pacesetter as she refers to her organization), in a previous chapter. Aviva and her team embrace the concept of growth through collaboration between employees and customers as a key focus and strength of their organization. "Our people are our conduit to growth," she said during our conversation about the continued growth of her organization in what is a highly competitive and commoditized market. Aviva and her leadership team have set out to ensure that every employee feels like they are part of Team Pacesetter; moreover, she understands the influence they have on both the organization and its customers. For example, Aviva ensures that all employees are exposed to "the organization's numbers," including revenue, expenses, and profits (amongst other key metrics). These are reviewed in detail, with discussions centered on how the entire team can influence these numbers, while continuing to be more innovative and supportive with customers. When I asked Aviva why she shared the numbers with all employees, rather than just with the senior leadership team, she said, "The more our team members know about how the organization is doing, the better positioned they are to influence the organization and the more ownership they will take in their role. And we don't hide anything either, we share everything—the good and the bad."

Aviva's ideas about sharing the numbers are a consistent approach taken by CEOs and executives of unstoppable organizations. I mentioned earlier as well the history of Jeff Sziklai, the CEO of Bellwyck Packaging Solutions. Jeff, since taking over the business from his father-in-law, still ensures that either he or a member of his executive team stop at each of the eight facilities they own every quarter to share the company's numbers: from profits to revenue to losses. In fact, every CEO that I met with or interviewed for this book shares a similar philosophy and approach when it comes to strategically sharing information with their employees and its value in supporting continued growth and profitability.

In a recent interview, Brad Smith, CEO of Intuit, said: "The pace of change today is unprecedented. Technology is evolving faster than ever and our employees need to keep pace with trends and strategy. To do that, we've increased our transparency so we can move faster—sharing information that was once only shared with the CEO. Trust and reputation are also more important than ever in today's connected world. We strive to build our reputation based on trust and respect, to attract and retain top talent."[3]

How Much Information is Too Much?

The question that I hear most frequently in response from CEOs and executives when I discuss the importance of sharing information with employees is, "Shawn, how much communication is too much?" This is a good question considering that for the most part we are all, including our employees, bombarded with information constantly, from e-mails to calls to meetings. In fact, one might think that all of this communication and information sharing only serves to only reduce employee productivity. But this perception is wrong because in essence it's not the volume of communication that matters; it's the quality that counts.

Our employees may be bombarded with e-mails, messages, and meetings, but we have to ask ourselves: What value does this information bring to them? Does it help them to be more effective in their job? Does it contribute to building their decision-making abilities so as to empower them in their role? Do the meetings they attend provide additional information that they can actually put to use?

In my experience, they often don't.

When I was working for a large power generation company about 15 years ago, I was leading a team that ranged in size from 12 to 32 people, depending on the types of projects and time of year. As I was also the lead for our group within one of the generating stations, I was expected to attend all of the meetings as a "representative" of my department, acting as a conduit in communication. As more people became aware of my presence, and the contributions I brought, my schedule became fraught with meetings. I was literally in meetings every day from 7:30 a.m. until 2 or 3 p.m., with some days extending until 5 p.m. I'm all for collaboration, but the schedule (and the pace I had to sustain to make it from one meeting to another on time) was ridiculous. The more time I spent in meetings, the less time I was available for my team, which also meant that they weren't as productive as they could be, often holding back on or delaying projects to await my feedback, ideas, or support. Something had to change and quickly, if I was going to succeed in leading my team. I decided to triage my meeting schedule, focusing on my priorities and ensuring that the development of my team in the process took precedence. This is an approach I've used in coaching executives and leaders many times in the years since. It's a tool that helps leaders at all levels of an organization identify how to prioritize their communication interactions to avoid burnout and being overwhelmed.

The approach is as follows.

1. Identify priorities in order of importance.
2. Identify key stakeholders who influenced my role and that of my team.
3. Identify critical projects/assignments that required my focus and involvement.
4. Identify delegates who could also represent our department or team in different areas of specialty.
5. Communicate the new system to everyone involved and deal with any fall-out.

Here is an example of what my plan entailed.

My priorities:

- Provide mentorship and support to my team.
- Act as a liaison for the department.
- Ensure critical projects for the department continue to move forward.

Key stakeholders:

- Senior management.
- Maintenance and operations.
- Engineering.

Critical projects/assignments (priorities at the time my plan was created):

- Full ERP implementation.
- Inventory optimization.
- Warehouse layout optimization.

Delegates within the team:

- John Taylor – Union Team Lead
- Bob Albright – Senior Employee
- Katie Bright – New Employee
- Stacey Smith – Tooling Specialist

Communication plan:

- Discuss plan with team members for input and buy-in.
- Review plan with vice president for feedback and buy-in.
- Communicate plans to key stakeholders, including the impacts on meetings.

To obtain a blank copy of this plan, visit *www.unstoppable organization.com* and download one for your own use or that of your team.

The pushback I received from others who were on the receiving end of my plan, following a reduction in my personal attendance and participation in meetings, interestingly, didn't come from executives or my team itself, but instead from various other employees and leaders from across the business who wanted me to personally attend all of their meetings. When I pushed back, first determining if attending would provide value to our department, then assessing if it did, and who would be the most appropriate to attend (a development opportunity for future leaders of the team and department), those setting up meetings or calls would invariably become irritated at my seeming lack of willingness to participate.

What I found through this experience is that there are three different default approaches people tend to apply when needing to communicate within an organization, namely:

1. Hold a meeting.
2. Hold a remote meeting (for example, a conference call or through Skype).
3. Send an e-mail.

There are variations of these three methods that were often used, but I found that most people tended to prefer one approach for virtually all of their outward bound communications, rather than identify the best approach based on what was to be communicated and who required the information. More specifically, people who preferred sending e-mails rarely booked meetings, and in turn, people who preferred meetings rarely used e-mails. The individual preferences of employees tended to guide their mode of communicating, rather than assessing each communication individually and then determining how best to respond. What I found was that when I pushed back on an approach identified by the communicator (for example, not able to attend their meeting, participate on their call, or respond or acknowledge their e-mail), many of these people would become frustrated or even angry with me for not conforming to their needs or expectations based on the perception that how they preferred to communicate was the best option (further validating our earlier discussions around how each person assesses value individually).

I share this story because there are some key lessons to be learned from this situation that most organizations are plagued with today; by overcoming or resolving these issues, we can better understand how much communication is too much. To begin, I often outline the following in many of the talks that I deliver to senior leaders. I call these the Five Rules to Effective Communications for Leaders:

1. Communication is a dialogue, not a monologue. Any communication that is of value must include participation and feedback from those involved, otherwise it adds no value.

2. People absorb information in predominantly one of three ways: kinesthetic, audio, and visual, often having a primary and secondary preference that they are not aware of. Any communication that does not support the absorption of information on all three levels is ineffective.

3. To ensure communication has value and relevance, it must be prioritized. There is such a thing as too much communication when it doesn't serve to add value. If you've ever sat on a conference call and pushed mute in order to get work done, you've tuned out. This is most often a result of a combination of numbers 1, 2, and 3.

4. Meetings and calls should be built around objectives, not time constraints. Just because Outlook suggests meeting times in 30-minute blocks does not mean a meeting can't take 16 or 42 minutes. In fact, building a meeting around time rather than objectives often creates a habit of filling time, rather than focusing on objectives.

5. If the objectives of the larger group (in this case the plant) do not align, then departmental objectives and those of individuals within the department will conflict. Creating broad objectives that stretch from the top of the organization down, and align from the bottom up, are key to ensuring everyone is focused and that communications have and add value.

When it comes to ensuring every communication adds value to its intended audience, we return to the practice we mentioned earlier in this chapter in which top performing CEOs understand and practice a habit of sharing business performance information with their people. Why do they do this? Because the information:

- Has relevance and value for everyone if positioned correctly.
- Helps to connect individual performance with organizational performance.
- Influences behaviors and employee buy-in to projects and assignments that are critical.
- Provides a platform to communicate frontline employee issues and concerns with senior management.
- Creates consistency in messaging—everyone gets the same information at the same time.
- Quashes opportunities for rumors or hearsay as it pertains to the performance of the organization.
- Builds a foundation for measuring employee performance against business objectives.

In my experience, what CEOs eventually realize is that communication is a tool that drives attention, awareness, and focus, which is what I realized many years ago. If you were to sit in on the presentations that Aviva holds with her team, for example, you would find that the information is geared toward the audience, what they understand and see as valuable, and that the discussions she holds are very much a dialogue with her team, not a monologue. She could just send out an e-mail, or have department managers and leaders roll the information down to employees, but Aviva recognizes that for information to add value and be relevant, it needs to come from her and the senior leadership team directly in the form of a dialogue. She also recognizes that it needs to be done in a setting that facilitates discussion because it's through discussion that understanding evolves.

Communication as a Conduit to People

As we discussed in an earlier chapter when meeting Aviva Leebow Wolmer, CEO of Pacesetter Steel, the sharing of business information in a face-to-face dialogue with employees is critically important as it's through these dialogues she is able to empower her associates, enabling them to make the right decisions in a timely manner. Aviva recognizes what many CEOs and senior managers do—that your employees cannot be effective in their roles in offering value to customers if they lack the knowledge and information to do so. Interestingly, the commonality amongst these CEOs is not just that they share information frequently with their teams, but also in the other not-so-subtle approaches they consistently practice to ensure that communication that flows throughout the organization has value for employees:

- They communicate face-to-face, using e-mail only as a supportive tool to provide further context or support for their discussions.
- They involve their executive team in the presentation, ensuring that the communication is a team effort.
- They incorporate a question-and-answer period in every dialogue with their people, allowing employees to discuss their concerns and for senior leaders to hear them first-hand.
- They don't avoid tough questions, but rather face them head-on recognizing if one person has a concern, it likely echoes the concerns of others.
- They walk the halls and floors of their organizations before and after the discussions, allowing for further one-on-one or group dialogue where it might make sense to have such.

More importantly, this approach to their communications doesn't stop at the executive level, but rather rolls down throughout the organization. In private with their executive teams, these leaders hold open dialogues on a frequent basis, avoiding e-mail wherever possible. They also ensure that department managers, supervisors, and team leaders also hold frequent (often daily) face-to-face team meetings, through a dialogue focused on the day's or week's objectives.

In fact, the most common practice among the CEOs I interviewed was communicating through dialogue. At Pacesetter Steel, Aviva ensures that all leaders across the organization practice both group and individual coaching sessions, as she refers to them, to guarantee that face-to-face dialogues occur regularly.

At this point, you might be wondering how the advent and evolution of technology that we referenced earlier is influencing these seemingly old-school communication practices. After all, with all of the texting, online chats, and instant messaging options, as well as visual communication tools such as Skype and Zoom, why would we even need to hold face-to-face meetings? In addition, don't most of the younger generations prefer communication via technology versus face-to-face dialogue? The answer, according to Aviva, is complicated. Yes, younger generations prefer to incorporate technology into their communications more than older generations, but technology simply can't and won't replace the value of having face-to-face communications. Aviva should know, after all, because she is a Millennial. Through her own development and experiences as a CEO, Aviva knows that the clichés around Millennials are often false, driven by perceptions that evolve from misunderstanding or misinterpretation. It's true that the Millennial generation has grown up with more exposure to technology that supports communication. However, it's also true that this generation, soon to be the largest working one in North America, has also grown up in and become accustomed to a more collaborative environment, in school, sports, and even home life, than any previous generation. Their often-insatiable appetite for information, and to communicate and contribute, is often driven by this learned collaborative behavior. So if you believe that face-to-face communication to discuss organizational challenges and opportunities is only relevant to some of the older generations, think again.

In my own experience, it's this lack of clarity around when to communicate with technology versus other, more intimate forms such as face-to-face that tends to cause confusion and disengagement of employees in most organizations (consider my earlier example of how personal preferences guide our desires for how we communicate). Instant messaging or online chats were never meant to replace communications as we know them (although the companies selling the software might hope so!), but rather supplement them. This confusion seems to grow out of varying generations in the workplace having preferences in how to communicate; in turn, these preferences form biases from which CEOs and executives communicate.

I did some consulting with a mid-sized, privately held organization last year in which I interviewed nearly 30 employees of all ages and demographics and asked, "How can communications be further improved?" The number one response I received from the interviewees was a desire for more group meetings held by the CEO, by about 95 percent of respondents, with the remaining 5 percent having no comment or further ideas beyond what was already happening (which included the CEO's quarterly meetings). Interestingly, when I asked what technology employees found to be unnecessary, more than 80 percent of the employees aged 35 to 58 felt there was too much technology already in place, versus the 60 percent of those under that age who believed more technology should be introduced and used in order to minimize face-to-face meetings. The survey demonstrated that, amongst other points we've discussed already, technology is more desirable by those younger and presumably more comfortable with it, whereas more senior employees who may have had less experience with some of the technology believed it had a diminishing impact on the value and relevance of communication. More specifically, the results clearly demonstrated the following:

1. Communications with the CEO and executive team had the greatest impact on employee morale and engagement.
2. Technology was a key component to communication, if properly defined for how it might supplement existing communications.
3. Effective training and introduction of technology to support communications was crucial to buy-in and proper application.

4. Generational demographics were directly proportional to the degree of buy-in and acceptance of technology use and application in the workplace.

The results demonstrate my earlier point. Too many organizations and the executives and leaders within them are looking toward new technology as a replacement for face-to-face communications, rather than treating it as a tool that can be used to supplement them. This is not to say that technology doesn't have a place in workplace communications today—quite the contrary. However, if you truly want to engage your employees in understanding the business, its customers, and more importantly, the role they play in adding value to the customer's experience, then face-to-face communication between executives and employees is the key.

What to Communicate and When

Structuring how to best communicate in order to be relevant and valuable to employees, then, is just as important as the information that is communicated. As discussed earlier in this chapter, having meetings and sending e-mails for the sake of satisfying personal preferences often diminishes employee interest and engagement in what is being communicated. Drawing on the earlier example with Aviva and her team, the key to success in communicating between senior leaders and frontline employees is frequency, consistency, and transparency. More specifically:

Frequency: A planned communication between senior leadership and frontline employees across the organization should happen quarterly at a minimum, or monthly to a maximum. Too few dialogues result in a loss for context in the conversations, whereas too frequent dialogues result in less than valuable information being shared just to fill time.

Consistency: Once you start holding dialogues with employees, sharing business and customer information, it's important that you continue to do so consistently. Creating consistency leads to employees anticipating the discussions, and in turn preparing for them. Consistency also demonstrates a commitment to the value of the dialogue itself, setting aside the various other priorities for the CEO, executives, and the organization, creating in essence a culture of accountability.

Transparency: The key to having dialogues that are deemed both valuable and interesting is in being transparent. Aviva dives deeply with her management team into the numbers to discuss impacts on the business and its operations, and provides a similar but broader overview (with less detail) to associates. She ensures that she is transparent with both groups, and that the information fielded in conversations is valuable and meaningful. Her key ingredient is transparency, openly answering questions directly and sharing with all of the associates from across the business.

Based on this approach and my interviews with a dozen CEOs of unstoppable organizations, there are clear similarities in the types of information shared with employees, which includes:

- Financial performance, including profits, operating expenses, and revenue losses.
- Customer issues and feedback on products or services.
- Investments into the business, regardless of cost and complexity.
- Customer news that includes new customers coming on board and those who have decided to leave.
- Changes in the marketplace and the impact of market and political forces on the business.
- Updates on competitors and the changes in product or service offerings.

To ensure that all employees fully understand and absorb the information shared, all of the CEOs I have interviewed say that they include slides (for visual listeners), dialogue (for audible listeners), and question and answer periods (for kinesthetic listeners). They also often follow up on these discussions with smaller break-out sessions, typically held within one week of the broader discussion, in which frontline leaders have more intimate discussions with employees on what they heard, and what they as a team can do to further improve the circumstance. In Aviva's case, recognizing that visual cues play an important role in communication, her team has created large vision boards in each department, providing an open area for employees to note their own ideas for improvement, ensuring that any ideas that evolve after the meetings or that may have been misunderstood during them are not lost. "It's all about providing employees with various avenues upon which to communicate," said Aviva while discussing the vision board concept.

Lessons from Unstoppable Organizations

Despite the hustle and bustle of life in most businesses today, unstoppable organizations and their leaders recognize that information shared with employees is power. They use communication strategies to share information with employees throughout the organization, such as:

- Open dialogues in a face-to-face environment with their employees.
- Information shared in a transparent manner, and catering it to its specific audience.
- Technology used as a tool to supplement important communications, rather than replace them.
- Meetings and agendas being set around objectives and not time.
- Group meetings, one-on-one meetings, and various open forums allowing employees to provide feedback and ideas in the form they choose when they choose.

6

DEALING WITH THE "ME" GENERATION

And I know that the younger generation is doing things that are so ingenious. And for them it's not a matter of a political belief or an environmental stance. It's really just common sense.

Daryl Hannah, Author

Further to our discussions in Chapter 5, communication is central to an unstoppable organization, not just in frequency but in the value information shared has for employees in understanding how they can contribute to and add value to their customers. If you've ever invested any time in improving communications either within your team or across the organization, then invariably you've stumbled upon some challenges in finding the right mix and approach to communicating that satisfies all employees. As we've alluded to previously, it's the individuality of employees that makes the task of communicating effectively such a challenge. In today's organizations, age demographics can typically range from employees who are just starting in their career and in their early 20s to those nearing the end of their career, and often in their late 60s or even early 70s. With such a wide spread in age, for leaders to select a single approach to communication as their primary preference such as face-to-face meetings, e-mail, or texting, the result can actually be detrimental to the culture, creating conflict, barriers to collaboration, and in the worst case, unplanned attrition or departure. All of this occurs despite the leader's best intentions in wanting to communicate effectively with their team.

Before we dive too deep into a discussion on generational differences and preferences, however, let me note now that neither this book nor what I'm about to discuss is meant as another "Let's roast the Millennial generation" rant. In the speaking that I do around North America on the topic of generational differences, the one thing that audience members of all ages tell me they can relate to is that our preferences for how we communicate are influenced mostly by our experiences as individuals, and are not simply the result of what our generation suggests is the required norm. Recognizing the relevance of this statement sheds light on some of the "issues" or "complaints" I often hear from CEOs and executives about their people, such as:

Younger employees always want to text and never pick up the phone when something's important!

There is too much e-mail floating around; why don't people just pick up the telephone?

There are too many meetings that are absorbing employees' time; why do we need so many meetings?

Our younger employees spend all of their time with their heads buried in their phones, rather than on their work!

Before we begin discussing the various idiosyncrasies and, in some instances, biases for each generation, let's be clear on some terminology I'll be referencing in this chapter, specifically understanding the range of dates in which each generation was born, and the significant events that occurred during these periods that influenced their perceptions, experiences, and values. For it is these very events, according to research by such organizations as the Association for Physiological Science[1], that have influenced and created the perspectives and ideals of each generation.

Considering the demographic of those still actively working today, let's begin with a brief definition of the Baby Boomer generation, who are generally identified as being born between the years 1945 and 1964.[2] Events that occurred during the younger and more influential years of this generation included the assassination of President John F. Kennedy, the first landing on the moon, and the fall of the Berlin wall.

Generation X are those generally born between 1965 and 1980, with significant events such as the rise in popularity of personal computers, the HIV epidemic, Y2K, and the dotcom boom which influenced this generation's perceptions.[3]

Generation Y, otherwise known as Millennials, are those born between 1981 and 2005. They have been influenced by events such as 9/11, the rise in availability and influence of social media, smart phones, etc.[4]

Generation Z, those born after 2000, are still evolving as I write this book, and most are not yet in the workforce full-time. Notably, this generation has been influenced by technology and the continuing disruption of what have, in many cases, become recognized as long-standing institutions or practices. Consider, for example, that it's more than likely this generation will not be as accustomed to using taxis, and are more likely to use ride sharing as a major form of transportation. As this generation is currently just entering the workforce, there have been few studies relative to generational influence or preferences.

There's a reason I'm purposefully not spending much time defining each of these generations, and I will spend even less time discussing what might or might not be as a result of generational preferences. In my experience, the ability of an organization to become unstoppable has little to do with the generations that are working for it. The issues we perceive to be "Millennial" or "Baby Boomer" issues (Generation X seem to slide under the radar most of the time for some reason, more than likely because it is most versed with understanding and adapting to both Millennials and Baby Boomers) are in fact those that relate less to the age demographic and more to a lack of understanding people. It's time that we learned to identify with these distinctions as direct biases, and recognize that the preferences that each generation have are simply individual differences that can differ between anyone of any age. For example, I've actually found some Baby Boomers who prefer texting, just like I've found some Millennials who enjoy picking up the phone or having a face-to-face discussion over texting. Instead, we need to focus on what we already know to be the case when it comes to our employees being effective in their roles, namely:

1. Engagement of our customers and employees results from communications that are in line with each *individual's* preferences. Therefore, the best method to communicate with each person regardless of their generation is by offering and using a medium for communication that meets each individual's preference. By doing so, you increase your chances that this particular individual will open up and have a dialogue with you. Generational differences are a component of our personal preferences, but are not the sole measure by which we can assess or value other people.

2. Communication preferences that individuals have include both personal and professional experiences and influences. A Millennial may be highly focused on texting due to how their parents, friends, and teachers have communicated with them, whereas someone else of the same age may prefer to use Snapchat or Facebook as a result of how their parents, teachers, and friends communicated with them. The commonality is technology, but the method and degree by which technology is incorporated will be influenced based on exposure, knowledge, and comfort. According to Pew Research, for example, 88 percent of Facebook users in the United States are between the ages of 18 and 29, 84 percent are between 30 and 49, 72 percent are between the ages of 50 and 64, and 62 percent are ages 65 and older.[5] At face value (no pun intended), this would suggest that the older someone is (which is directly related to their generation), the less likely they are to engage on social media. However, in making this statement we are forming a generalization based on research and, while it's quite possible that generational influences are at play, it would be ridiculous to suggest that anyone over the age of 65 isn't involved in or understands Facebook.

3. Because we literally spend more waking hours at a place of work than anywhere else (when employed full-time), the workplace can actually have a significant influence on individual preferences through time. Therefore, it can be expected that, with time, the communication methods employed by and within an organization can reshape how we

prefer to communicate. For example, my first cell phone was a Blackberry[6] that I was issued as a "tool" for work use back in 2001. As I grew more comfortable with using the phone, I also began to explore the various ways I could use it, including sending messages and using some of the popular applications. Within a couple of years I purchased a Blackberry for my own personal use, eventually transitioning to an iPhone. Today, it is likely those entering the workforce already have a smartphone. But when the technology was first introduced and my employer at the time decided to adopt it for their employees, the result influenced how I prefer to communicate in my personal life outside of work.

Where to Find Your Customers

Understanding the generational differences as just described provides us with some context as to "why" there are different preferences for various ages in how they interact and communicate with others. Although the Millennial generation is heavily engaged in technology, and therefore consider it as key to supporting their ongoing communications (texting, social media), it doesn't mean they are unable to use or adapt to face-to-face communications. In the teaching I have done in recent years as an adjunct professor at Humber Polytechnic College[7], I've learned that the Millennial generation is one of the most engaged while in a face-to-face group setting. This generation has been raised with greater exposure to teams and encouraged more than previous generations during their education to collaborate with one another. Similarly, as I mentioned earlier, Aviva Leebow Wolmer, CEO of Pacesetter Steel, is herself a Millennial and she is leading an organization that consists of three different generations. During our discussions, Aviva said that the biases about how Millennials prefer to communicate are most often false: "Millennials are actually very engaged in the workplace and highly adaptive to a group setting, though only if those discussions are deemed by them as valuable, important, and inclusive of their ideas and feedback." Building on Aviva's point, the Millennial generation may actually be more productive and effective in a face-to-face setting than previous generations. Whereas the Baby Boomer generation grew up in an era where speaking up to share ideas was done at the risk of being interpreted as talking back or out of turn, the Millennial generation has been encouraged throughout their lives to share their ideas openly, which is a breath of fresh air for many executives and leaders.

Despite the fact that generational differences are a component of understanding the unique differences and preferences of our employees and customers, one thing is for certain. We are in the midst of a growing shift amongst all generations to be more involved and reliant on the Internet. Unstoppable organizations are keenly aware that their reputation and relationships online for both their existing and potential employees, as well as their existing and prospective customers, are becoming increasingly important to their success. Welcome to the "online generation."

To put this into perspective, let's begin by considering the influence the Internet is having on today's customers and, in turn, on our employees. Then we will discuss how unstoppable organizations are adapting to and capitalizing on these shifts. Starting with our customers, let's look at some recent statistics across all generations relative to how many customers are moving online to inform or make their purchases:

- 72 percent of Millennials research and shop their options online before going to a store or the mall.[8]
- Two-thirds of Americans over the age of 50 buy from e-retailers online.[9]
- More than three-quarters of adults surveyed in the United States had ordered products or services online. And whereas Millennial adults (ages 24 to 32) are the most likely to have done so, Gen Xers (ages 33 to 46) spend the most.[10]
- Digital interactions influence 36 cents of every dollar spent in the retail store, or approximately $1.1 trillion total.[11]
- 84 percent of store visitors use their mobile devices before or during a shopping trip, with 22 percent of consumers spending more as a result of using digital. Just more than half of these shoppers report spending at least 25 percent more than they had intended. And 75 percent of respondents said product information found on social channels influenced their shopping behavior and enhanced loyalty.[12]

I selected these statistics to shed some light on the points we've been discussing so far in the chapter; that customers of all generations are being influenced and choosing to purchase online is not a "Millennial thing." This influence is driven by the availability of technology, as well as the ease of accessibility to the Internet, with Wi-Fi an almost expected norm by most people in North America today. In turn, this allows customers to perform more research at lightning speed before ever deciding to make a purchase.

There are a few important points we can derive from this research that unstoppable organizations have not only recognized, but repeatedly acted on to ensure they can keep up with and appeal to their customers, namely:

1. All companies, be they in retail, distribution, manufacturing, or services need to have a reputable presence online. Trying to figure out how to build a Website yourself, or having your neighbor's kid who is apparently "a wiz at this stuff" build one, is not a wise choice considering the number of potential and existing customers who might visit it.

2. Having an online presence for the sake of "keeping up with the competition" is insufficient. If you are going to be online (and you should be!), then your online presence needs to be dynamic, not static. Simply having a Website or a Facebook page representing your organization without consistently and meaningfully engaging with those who come across your online presence can be more detrimental than helpful to your customer relationships.

3. When it comes to helping customers and employees find you, nothing outweighs the benefits of being omnipresent. There are so many ways for customers to find products and services online today; the key is to understand how your customers are typically searching for your organization's products or services, and then be present, ready, and waiting to engage with them. You can use free means to gain their attention such as LinkedIn, Facebook, Twitter, Instagram, blogs, and press releases. Or you can gain their attention through paid means such as increasing your searchability by investing in SEO (search engine optimization) services for your Website, or using online advertisers such as Google AdWords. The key is to be everywhere your customers might be, and once you're there be ready to have a conversation.

4. Facilitate an easy transaction. Allowing your customers to buy directly from you through the use of an online shopping cart only makes sense. At a minimum, you should offer a way for customers to obtain a quote without forcing them to contact you via your organization's preferred means (for example, e-mail) in order to make an investment. If a customer is ready to buy online, then you should offer them the ability to do so.

5. Be responsive. Similar to allowing your customers the opportunity to buy directly from you, make sure that your online presence is something that is monitored and managed closely. There is nothing worse for a customer than launching an online chat feature, only to find there is no one on the other end or the wait times are excessive.

Several years ago, I did some consulting work for a large distributor of industrial supplies. At the time, the distributor was struggling to remain profitable (never mind grow!) and wanted help in assessing how they could right their "ship" and grow the business. They knew it was possible because their competition was continually capturing more and more of their market share. Initially, I met with dozens of employees and customers to assess the situation. Next, I reviewed their marketing material, which included their online presence. Although the company was highly reputable and had been around for decades, their online presence and related online marketing was dismal. Most alarming was the fact that although you could review in detail the specs for virtually all of their products online, there was no pricing presented, and you could not purchase any of their products online; rather, you must contact someone via e-mail to provide you a price and support your making a purchase. In interviewing several of their key customers, mostly plant and maintenance managers, interviewees kept mentioning that they preferred the competition's Website because they could, when it was convenient for them, select what they needed and buy the product, rather than wait to hear back from an e-mail inquiry before buying. Time was of the essence and an online shopping cart helped key customers reduce the time it took to purchase products. It was put best by one maintenance manager of a multinational company who said, "Look, I do most of my maintenance planning after 4 p.m., which means I'm typically looking to order parts after 5 p.m. [The distributor] is only open until 4:30 p.m. daily, which forces me to make a list and e-mail it in, waiting on a response which often comes by around noon the next day. Instead of that, I could go to their competition, select the same products online, buy them online, and have them delivered by noon the next day. Which distributor would you rather use?"

Concerned, I took this information directly to the CEO and vice president of sales who had hired me, suggesting that an online shopping cart and pricing needed to be introduced on the Website right away if they were to stop their competition from taking business. The CEO wholeheartedly disagreed with me, saying, "As soon as I put my prices online, my competitors can see them or they can be shared. The risk is too high!" Needless to say, this distributor is no longer in business today, a mere five years later. None of my recommendations were taken. My point here is simple. Engaging with customers online is only going to continue to grow with time, as proven recently by a Forrester study which found that online retail sales are predicted to grow from USD $231 billion in 2012 to USD $370 billion in 2017.[13]

Customers: Get Online or Inline

To help you prepare for either moving some or more of your business activities online in order to satisfy your customers, here is an exercise I use with many of my clients to assess their online presence and its value to their customers, both existing and prospective. Ask these questions of five of your existing customers and five of your potential customers (or those of your competitor):

1. How do you search for (insert product/service) currently? If this does not include online sources, would the availability of such help make your research easier and better?

2. Of these means, which do you find most credible? If online is not on the shortlist, why not? What could we do to make your online search for our product/service more credible?

3. Once you've completed your research, how do you prefer to purchase the product/service? If online, how user friendly do you find our Website and social media page? If not online, would it being online make your decision easier?

4. What could we do to help us stand out from our competitors online (for example, our Website, social media, searchability, and chat features)?

5. How willing would you be to share your online experience with others through rating our product/service or providing a testimonial? What could we do to entice you to share your experience?

For bonus questions and other supportive materials, make sure you visit *www.unstoppableorganization.com.*

Feedback to these questions will help you determine the extent to which your current online presence, features, and functionality are attractive to your ideal customers, and will also shed some light on where you may want to invest more time or money to guarantee your online presence is appealing. It is also important to ensure you are engaging not just your typical customer, but also potential future customers. This is an opportunity to become crystal clear on what your future customer (or generations of future customers) is seeking in an organization that provides your product or services. Additionally, this ensures that any investments you make in time or money to further bolster your online presence is in fact directed by your customers, rather than based on feedback from your IT department.

Bob Nadon, President of Upper Canada Stretcher, a provider of custom-made stretchers for canvas and related products to support the art community, was faced with this daunting task upon launching his business in a small rural community. Bob loved living in the area, and wanted to stay away from the hustle and bustle of the big city. Bob realized, however, that in order to reach his end customer, artists, he needed to build and grow his online presence. Having launched a Website, Bob and his team recognized that to grow their organization they needed to support not only distributors of their products, but to reach and support their end users directly. Through several calculated changes, Bob and his team built an easy to use and highly functional Website, allowing end users multiple options to purchase custom or stock products, either in person (exchanging e-mails or phone calls), or directly online through an online shopping cart. By focusing on a direct route to his customers by incorporating technology at an early stage of his business, Bob has been able to ensure customers receive responsive service for their high quality products. A thriving organization with customers from across North America and overseas, Bob and his team have taken an alternative route to the typical manufacturer by offering online sales directly to their end customer, and as a result his business continues to grow on an annual basis.

Like Upper Canada Stretchers or other organizations I've mentioned thus far, what's important for future success is to be where your customers are, and a growing number of your customers, regardless of their age, are online.

Preparing for a Growing Generation of Employees Online

Understanding how your customers are moving online, however, is only one piece of the puzzle when it comes to building an unstoppable organization. The other piece includes considering that in order to attract and retain the best employees who will serve your customers online or otherwise, an organization must also appeal online to its existing and potential employees.

I recently validated this perceived shift during a lecture on career planning with a group of university graduates. When a student asked me how I suggested they go about finding a good job, I asked, "Tell me, what process are you following today?" The responses from the class of nearly 40 students were generally the same, in the following sequence:

1. Look at online job opportunities on Websites such as Monster and LinkedIn.
2. Research the company by reviewing their Website and presence on LinkedIn.
3. If the company and job appeared to fit the candidate's desires for an employer (with skills being a secondary consideration), they would apply by e-mail or through a Website.
4. They collectively confirmed that at this point they would wait, sending the odd e-mail follow-up, eventually giving up after three or four e-mails sent with no response.

These responses suggest something similar to our discussion on customers moving online; that is, that the employees of today (and tomorrow) are seeking out jobs and planning for their career online rather than through friends, the newspaper, or physical job boards. Similarly, having an out-of-date Website, poor Internet ranking, bad Google reviews, or a weak social media presence can influence the potential employee in steps 1 or 2 just outlined. Moreover, these potential candidates were being selective about who they applied to, with the company's values (what they stood for) and future vision (where they are going) being key identifiers of preferred versus undesirable employers.

The comfort level with using the Internet doesn't stop with how employees seek out job opportunities, however. It also includes their willingness (and ability) to rate their employers online, providing a virtual "heads-up" to other potential job seekers as to what their interpretation is of their employer, its leadership, culture, or any other aspect they wish to discuss or rant about. Sites such as *www.glassdoor.com*, *www.vault.com*, and *www.hallway.com* are popping up all over the Web, allowing employees (and even prospective employees who have had an interview or interaction with someone at the organization) to anonymously post their experiences, perceptions, and beliefs regarding any company or person within a company that they so choose. Have an interview and you were impressed or ticked off about how the interview went? Just log in and post your thoughts on these Websites with no worries about being found out. Super happy about your boss and how she helps you? Just log in and post away. Frustrated you didn't get a raise this year? Log in and talk about it. The options and opportunities are virtually endless, and what this means to employers is that monitoring and managing your online presence has never been more important.

But when trying to attract great employees, it's more than just about managing your online presence. Unstoppable organizations recognize that in order to prepare for attracting and accepting their future employees, they must recognize what these employees desire or demand of their future employers.

Zappos, the former online shoe company purchased by Amazon but still overseen by the founder Tony Hsieh, bucks the historically popular methods of attracting and hiring talent. Instead, they allow applicants to become "insiders," connecting with Team Ambassadors who get to know them before ever considering an interview or the possibility of hiring. As the relationship evolves, insiders are brought to Zappos headquarters, typically met by a driver who is, in fact, a Zappos employee. The employee reports back to the ambassador about their experiences with the insider, how they were treated, and details about the interaction. This approach is seen as the cornerstone of Zappos hiring. As Tony put it during an interview, Zappos "only wants to hire people that treat their co-workers with respect."[14]

Alternatively, we could look at the hiring practices of Dyson, known best for their vacuum cleaners. A company highly focused on R&D, Dyson hires high school students rather than university graduates, placing them in R&D centers accompanied by lectures from seasoned professors. This work/study program not only provides students with an opportunity to learn in real life, but also the chance to earn a bachelor's degree while they learn.

When it comes to unique and engaging means to attract talent, particularly future talent who have been brought up with different ideas on the value of collaboration and the role technology can play in communication, unstoppable organizations such as Zappos and Dyson identify unique ways to connect their needs as an organization with the needs of younger generations.

To satisfy and meet the needs of your existing and future customers and employees, consider the evolving preferences and values of today's and tomorrow's generations. Don't get stuck in making decisions based on generational biases, but rather interview and interact with both your existing and future customers to understand what they desire of your organization, its products, services, culture, values, and leadership. Technology plays a significant role in this process, of course, but becoming aware of and incorporating customer and employee feedback is the first step toward becoming an unstoppable organization.

Lessons from Unstoppable Organizations

A growing segment of today's generations are online, using the Internet and technology to support most of their research and communication. As a result, unstoppable organizations recognize a need to have a powerful presence online to support and satisfy both customers and employees.

7

CREATING A CULTURE THAT ADDS VALUE TO YOUR CUSTOMERS

But change must always be balanced
with some degree of consistency.
Ron D. Burton, President, Rotary International

When it comes to attracting and retaining customers in today's increasingly online world, the CEOs, executives, and leaders who oversee unstoppable organizations are keenly aware that in order to grow and succeed (much less sustain their presence), they need to find, attract, and retain the right people. How, for example, can an organization with a longstanding presence in the marketplace, a strong brand presence, and quality products or services create consistently high value interactions with and for its customers if the very employees who are identifying and delivering this value aren't motivated to provide such or, worse yet, leaving the organization? Successfully satisfying the needs of today's customers can't be reasonably achieved if high turnover or low engagement of employees exists. If you haven't yet experienced this conundrum in your organization, you are either doing the right things or are lucky and luck has a time limit.

As we discussed in the previous chapters, today's younger generation in the workforce have different ideas about what their careers will be like, which influences their perceptions around loyalty to their employer. As I mentioned earlier, I don't make these statements to add to the cliché or biases around younger generations, but to point out changes in the perceptions of today's employees. A recent study conducted by Gallup[1] supports this fact and brings to life what many of the CEOs I interviewed already know to be true: the Millennial generation is a "job-hopping generation." Most notably, the study identifies that:

- Millennials are the most likely generation to leave their job.
- Six in 10 Millennials are open to the idea of a new job opportunity.
- Millennials are generally the least engaged generation in the workplace.

To put these statistics into perspective, the study found that 21 percent of Millennials have changed jobs in the last year, more than three times the number of non-Millennials that reported the same. In addition, only half of Millennials strongly agree that they plan to be working for their organization for the next year, which suggests that 50 percent are planning to leave within 12 months.

Now before you head down the halls screaming, let's put these statistics into perspective rather than take an extremist point of view (recall my earlier point about avoiding the tendency to create generalized statements from facts). Let me pose a few simple questions for you to reflect upon, based on your organization and its current state in regards to the mix of generations:

1. What is the current demographic of your workforce? Consider the percentage of young versus older workers.
2. What type of role does the predominance of each generation work in? Do you have a mixture of young and older

employees in each department, or are there areas in which there is a predominance of one generation or the other?

3. What are your current turnover statistics for the past 12 months? How many people have left, for what reasons, and how old were they?

4. What have you done as a result of feedback from those who have departed? Have you made any changes and, if so, have you communicated those changes to existing and potential employees?

5. What are your estimations for attrition in the coming 24 months? How many people are likely to retire (or leave for other reasons) and what are your plans for replacement (new hires versus existing employees)?

These questions are meant to provide two things. First, they will shed some light on the degree of risk that may exist within your organization relative to the impacts of employees departing. Second, and more importantly, they will shed light into what areas you need to address to build some plans for ensuring your organization will survive and thrive into the coming years based on the existing demographic of your employees. If, for example, you need new employees on account of attrition or customer growth, then these questions will give insight on what you need to incorporate into your workforce to ensure your organization continues providing value to its customers. Alternatively, if the levels of your staff are stable and there are no dramatic or foreseen changes (for example, those departing the organization) in the coming years, then the questions will shed light on the types of plans necessary in the coming years. What is important to realize from this exercise as well is that regardless of the current demographics within your organization, Millennials and Generation Z are soon to be the predominant generations amongst your employees. As a result, now is the time to consider what changes or improvements are necessary to appeal to these younger generations, but also to capitalize on the benefits they can bring to the organization as discussed earlier. You'll notice again I'm challenging you to think forward, a common theme amongst unstoppable organizations.

Virtually every one of the CEOs and executives that I've met and worked with, interviewed, and consulted prior to writing this book have confirmed that identifying new ways to support and engage with the workforce of tomorrow is top of their agenda when it comes to considering how to grow the organization and its revenue. Fortunately, many have found and introduced solutions that have supported lower turnover, higher interest in joining the organization from would-be employees, and higher, positive engagement from their existing employees, the combined results of which have led to stronger sales, more revenue, and increasing market share. Let's take a minute then to explore some of the ideas and changes that these unstoppable organizations have made, and the benefits they've achieved as a result.

Is it Too Little Too Late?

Mike Vokes, the President of Vokes Furniture, was faced with a challenge several years ago. As the demand for his custom crafted bedroom furniture grew, so did the number of employees he needed. This was despite the continued focus Mike placed on implementing lean practices to reduce waste and increasing automation to support higher productivity. As the number of employees grew, Mike had hired a plant manager to oversee daily operations. After just more than a year, it became clear that the plant manager was not working out for a variety of reasons. Mike realized that to engage with his employees on the level he knew was both necessary and possible (based on his early days working side by side with his people), he had to empower some of his senior team members to oversea plant operations, allowing them to oversee and lead their people, with Mike getting involved only when issues, ideas, or challenges became significant. This allowed Mike to remain engaged with his team, but giving the responsibility of managing each work area to someone familiar with it, and who had already gained respect from and built a strong relationship with the team. Since introducing these changes, the increased morale of Mike's employees, and most notably the continued dramatic growth of the organization (having near doubled in size), has proved the value of moving decision-making down to those engaged in the work.

In summary, what we can derive from Mike's lessons is that it's never too late to transition the organization toward a more empowered workforce, shifting decision-making to employees who in turn provide higher levels of employee engagement, which results in reduced turnover and increased productivity.

If Mike can make these changes amidst a business that has operated for nearly two decades in an industry that is known for high levels of competition and tight margins, then any organization can do the same. To consider your organization and its culture or operating practices as being set in stone or engrained into people to the extent that a change would fail is simply an excuse for avoiding making necessary changes that embrace the very benefits that younger generations bring with them. With this lesson in mind, logically the next obstacle is to determine where and how to begin. In fact, this is where I find many organizations stuck, committed to the change but unable to determine the best place to begin. To this I respond with an age old question: "How do you eat an elephant?" The answer, of course, is you eat an elephant one bite at a time.

Building a Culture of Employees Who Add Value to Your Customers

To create an environment and culture that appeals to your existing employees as well as younger generations requires a different way of thinking. As we learned through Mike's example, he has placed a continual focus on designing and deploying an effective model for leadership and mentorship, in combination with employing a tool such as the lean system that supports building a culture of continuous improvement. This is topped off by a consistent search for equipment and automation that further improves speed, quality, and consistency of products. Clearly, this is more than just about focusing on your people; however, you'll notice that what underlies all of these areas are people. Mike couldn't, for example, introduce a new saw if his employees weren't willing to embrace the new technology and adopt revisions to their existing processes. Employees underlie everything within an organization, and it's for that reason employees must be the priority.

It is no small feat, however, to consistently find new ways to tap into the creativity, ideas, and energy of today's younger generation while convincing them to embrace the experience of older generations and, in turn, converting all of this collaborative experience and knowledge into value for the customer that will support stronger revenue. The starting point then is considering your people as primary to success, and so ensuring that the teams throughout your organization are formed and trained in a way that capitalizes on their individual differences. This recognition results in what I call the golden rule to hiring; that is, team fit is more critical than individual skills when it comes to building an effective team, and more importantly, an effective organization.

As we've discussed previously, because the way that you add value to your customers is through your employees, then creating an environment in which employees are able and willing to add value is crucial. In earlier chapters we discussed the complexity of people, which extends to more than just generational considerations. The challenge then, as well as the opportunity, is creating an environment where employees understand, individually, the value that they bring to the organization and its customers and, in turn, how that value addresses your customers' needs. I've demonstrated this in the following figure:

FIG 7.1

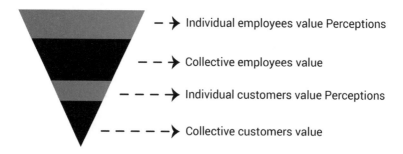

- → Individual employees value Perceptions

- - → Collective employees value

- - - → Individual customers value Perceptions

- - - - → Collective customers value

Let's first consider this diagram from the standpoint of a customer, and second from that of our employees.

Building an environment to attract employees means creating an organization that is clear about how they best add value to customers, both individually and collectively. With this clarity, supported by open communication through constant dialogue that flows from bottom up (from employees to leadership) as well as top down (from leadership to employees), the customer value chain (CVC for short) becomes a continuous process that ensures customers are always at the forefront of every employee's decisions and actions. There are different means to achieve a CVC, the most effective being combining several if not all of the following methods, including:

1. Clear definitions of how each role contributes first to customers and second to the organization, introduced and reviewed during hiring and employee review meetings.
2. Frequent meetings, both formal and informal, held between top leadership and employees, both individually and as a group to discuss evolving customer value and how the employee and their leader can meet these needs.
3. Cross-training practices that expose customer-facing employees (such as sales) to customer support roles (such as shipping) and vice versa, increasing awareness of the importance of the team in satisfying and adding value to customers.
4. Providing increased authority to employees to satisfy customer needs, ensuring leaders practice a "hands-off" approach to engaging with their people.
5. Using employee suggestion programs continuously, that are in turn supported and acted upon by organizational leaders.
6. Employee advisory panels that discuss and share ideas on current company challenges, presenting ideas and options to senior leaders for decision-making purposes.

Tony Solecki of Caframo, for example, sets aside time each week to meet one-on-one with his employees to discuss the current state of the organization, its customers, and the market, as well as requesting feedback from employees on they can be more effective in their roles. We've also discussed Jeff Sziklai at Bellwyck Packaging Ltd., who began the practice of quarterly reviews with all employees in which he would walk out onto the production floor and speak to them about the state of the business, including new opportunities and customer feedback. Jeff would then solicit ideas from employees to support the continued success of the business. The key in connecting employees to the value they can and do contribute to customers is communicating through dialogue. The options for doing this are endless, and as Mike from Vokes Furniture suggested earlier, there is no better time to start than now.

There are additional benefits to helping employees connect with the value they provide. These types of engagements allow for both employees and leaders to share their ideas, challenges, and opportunities based on their own experiences with customers. If a long-standing customer has been lost, senior management can share the feedback they received on why this happened. Alternatively, if employees have had feedback from a customer on something that needs to change, they can share this with management. The key to delivering value to the customer is to recognize that the ability to do so hinges on everyone's understanding of what customers are seeking, and how they as individuals can respond.

I mentioned the unstoppable success of Jeff and his team at Bellwyck Packaging. Their continued effort at satisfying a niche need for their customers was never an easy battle. Several years ago, a dominant competitor was trying to take a large customer account from Bellwyck by undercutting them on price. Always open with his team, Jeff shared details about the threat with his employees. He reassured everyone that the reason for the company's unstoppable success was that they were able to consistently turn around jobs within only a few days. Jeff emphasized that continuing to do this, while ensuring consistency and quality of their products, was the only way to keep this customer happy. As the CEO, Jeff knew that having every single employee focused on fast order turn-around was the only way to please this customer and thus sustain their business. In addition, Jeff asked his employees for ideas about what else could be done, and encouraged them to continue sharing ideas with him, the plant manager, or their supervisor if they came up with anything. Jeff's talks were very much a collaborative discussion that were both top-down and bottom-up, helping connect employees with the value that customers were seeking both strategically and tactically.

It's not only important, however, to ensure that every employee understands the specific value they offer through their role; they must also learn new ways of adding value. When I worked for Magna International, some 20-plus years ago now (gulp!), I worked as a logistics coordinator. I helped to organize and arrange for pickup of more than 160 outbound loads each day, working in a team of five other coordinators. After working in the role for about eight months, my boss Jim pulled me aside. "Shawn," he said, "you've got a great way of dealing with our customers when they have complaints or concerns. You track information well, make commitments that you keep, and always are able to determine the root cause so that solutions can be found to avoid the problem happening again. How would you like to take on the role of handling and overseeing all customer complaints?"

I was ecstatic about the chance for further responsibility so early in my career with Magna, and I've never forgotten that discussion with Jim. He always ensured that he connected my skills and accomplishments with supporting our customers, and where possible took full advantage of an individual's unique talents in order to help the organization, and more importantly, its customers. I should mention as well that the conversations Jim had with his team, similar to the one he had with me, weren't discussions that happened during an annual review, but rather were fluid. They could happen at any time if Jim received feedback or observed something good or bad. Jim was a master at helping his employees connect with how they benefited the customer, and he took full advantage of the individual skills and abilities of his people to further add value to his customers.

There are numerous ways that leaders can make these individual value connections with their employees, including:

1. Providing one-on-one feedback directly to employees on a frequent basis, sharing both positive and constructive feedback relative to the employee's role and actions on meeting customer needs. These do not have to be informal coaching sessions, but instead are a set agenda to ensure employees and supervisors stay focused on how the employee can add value.

2. Team discussions facilitated by a leader in which team members provide feedback on the influence others have on their work and, in turn, their collective value to customers. The basis of this dialogue, different from the previous example, is more focused on guided self-discovery on the influence employees have on customers, both directly and indirectly, with the leader simply facilitating the discussion rather than directly participating. By placing a group of employees together in a facilitated discussion to share insights and ideas about adding value to customers, the results can often be higher levels of receptivity by employees as compared to receiving feedback from a direct supervisor or manager,

which can sometimes fall on deaf ears or result in paranoia about job performance and stability.

3. Peer reviews amongst employees where internal employees provide feedback to their peers, sharing how their role and performance influenced them (as an internal customer for example) and openly discussing ideas about how to collectively improve value amongst one another to influence the end customer. This approach is more effective over the second example when teams are too large (for example, beyond 15 people) or too small (teams of two to three people) to hold a collective discussion. It is also effective when considering how to ensure dialogues are more meaningful. In a group setting, there is always a percentage of employees who will choose to remain relatively silent, requiring a highly skilled and trained facilitator.

For a printable version of these approaches in order to organize customer value chain discussions with your employees, make sure to visit *www.unstoppableorganization.com*.

Incorporating these types of dialogues into a leader's agenda, selecting one, or using all three in some fashion will ensure that employees consistently connect their roles and actions to satisfying individual and collective customer needs. In turn, this will add value to the customer's relationship with the organization, its products, or services. These can be effective tools when building and increasing awareness amongst existing employees. The question remains, however, if team fit is critical to building a customer-focused team, how do we achieve this when bringing on new hires?

Attracting and Hiring Employees Who Add Value

With a culture of employees highly focused on adding value, it might seem that all is well and good. Regardless of how unstoppable your organization is, the reality is employees will still come and go for a variety of reasons. From attrition to moving away, employee life changes will continue to influence their willingness and ability to stay at your place of employment. It's for this reason that how you attract and hire employees, ensuring you are careful about selection and integration, becomes critically important. Of course, the hiring practices of each organization can be different, depending on the sector in which you work, as well as policies and even legal requirements that may influence how and who you hire. For example, doctors, lawyers, and even those who work in trades have to meet specific educational and legal requirements to be hired for a job, to an extent that even the CEO or senior executive team has little or zero influence. For unstoppable organizations, however, it's not the criteria within which you hire employees, but the process you follow to ensure the employee you select is the right fit for your organization, the team they will be working with, and the customers they will interact with. Let's look at an example.

I worked with a client just over a year ago who led a marketing team. Hiring was a process that my client managed directly, although human resources provided some input. In essence, my client could hire who and how they wanted, as long as the hire possessed the basic skills and criteria for the role, typically set forth by HR, were met. Previously, my client had hired employees as most do, by reviewing and screening resumes, followed by one or two face-to-face meetings, resulting in selecting a candidate. My client found that integration and adoption of the "value first" mindset took time, with team members often not convinced that the candidate would be successful in the role, hence not investing much time or support in the early stages of probation to help the new employee succeed.

The issue, from my experience, was buy-in. Because employees on the team were not a part of the interview or hiring process, they remained cold to the person and at arm's length until they got to know the new employee personally, and became comfortable working with this person. This could take weeks or even months, particularly if the new employee was quiet or shy. We revised the hiring process to incorporate team involvement. The process for hiring looked like this:

Step 1: The job ad was reviewed by existing team members and relevant feedback (such as fit within the ad guidelines, etc.) was incorporated.

Step 2: The hiring department and my client, the vice president, screened new candidate's resumes. The dominant discussion points were on candidate experience and fit, tied back to how the new employee may assist the team in sustaining if not increasing the value added to existing and potential new customers or clients.

Step 3: A few candidates were interviewed. Two employees from the hiring team were involved (which the team self-selected or were drawn from a hat) and asked questions that the team was interested in, building on the already developed questions of the vice president and the hiring supervisor.

Step 4: Notes taken during the interview were first reviewed amongst the team of four, then summarized and taken back to the broader team for input and discussion, collectively agreeing on either a further short list of candidates for interview or to select a potential hire.

Step 5: The short list of candidates or the potential new hire were then invited in to meet with team members in their working environment, spending five to 15 minutes with at least four employees (different than those from the interview). Those employees the candidates met with were in roles that included a combination of people who were:

- In the same role as that of the potential new hire.
- In an internal customer role that the potential hire would be supporting and working with.
- In a role outside the hiring department, but were known to give open and honest feedback.

Step 6: Those who met with the candidates discussed their perceptions of the candidates, shared notes, thoughts, and ideas, with the goal of making a recommendation for hire to the vice president.

Step 7: A recommendation for hire was made and the selected candidate was contacted with the offer.

What were the benefits of this approach, you might wonder? Well, we definitely met our goal of ensuring new employees were embraced by the team faster. This approach guaranteed that employees who were already on the team bought into, and in turn had some responsibility for, the person hired to ensure their success. In addition, my client found the hiring process itself brought the team closer together, helping them to learn new ways to collaborate and share openly their ideas and feedback. Moreover, the process increased the tenure of new hires and reduced turnover, validating that those who were hired were more likely to not only be understood by their coworkers, but have a better feel for the role and their coworkers as well, making it more likely they would stick around.

Lastly, we identified our approach to hiring when creating job ads and letting others know the organization was hiring, making sure that potential candidates knew they would be meeting team members during their initial interview and have a chance (if placed on the short-list) of seeing their work area and meeting the rest of the team. Word got around about the approach, which meant more employees from other departments began to apply for internal positions, and externally there was an increase in the number of applicants.

The lesson is that unstoppable organizations increase their chances for success in hiring by involving their teams. In doing so, they make a closer and faster connection between new job candidates and that of their team members and internal and external customers, bridging the "value" gap on an individual and group level before candidates ever get hired.

Dealing With Employee Pushback and Inconsistency

Hiring using the approach just described ensures you select the right candidates, and can lead to an increase in the volume of applicants if word gets out. It's important to mention that shifting to such an environment with existing employees, where employees connect what they do with how they influence the value customers receive, isn't easy. There will always be those uncomfortable with the change for whatever reason, and it's important to recognize that some plans must be put into place to ensure a consistently high value interaction for your customers as you evolve through these changes. The last thing you want is an employee who isn't (at least initially) buying into your approach and, in turn, takes out their frustrations or doubts on your customers.

Moreover, until you have fully implemented and proven the processes just described, you may continue to experience employee turnover before the full impact of a value-based culture exists. In this instance, there are a few introductory measures that you need to take to stay on course.

First, make sure employees cross-train both inside their existing department as well as with other outside departments that influence their role. By doing so internal to the department, you guarantee a natural evolution of sharing best practices, in which employees either more senior or more skilled in specific areas share their processes and methods, and a natural collaboration occurs. Doing so externally increases the employees' awareness of how other departments and individuals function, once again ensuring a process of internal best practices where employees identify new means of performing in their roles that in turn can make other roles more productive or efficient.

One client who manufactured home products said there was a battle happening consistently between their customer service department and sales department, to the extent that customer service employees were leaving the business, frustrated at the lack of support. We instituted cross training that helped broaden the perspectives of both sales and customer service on the idiosyncrasies of each of their roles, as well as ensured they shared differing perspectives from their interactions with customers. This only helped to increase the customer value awareness of both the departments as well as the individuals within each group.

Second, capture key processes in a simple form. In essence, draft procedures and best practice cheat sheets, but make sure the documents are created and managed by the employees who use them, not an external department or someone who is at arm's length from the work. Keep the practice simple to ensure documents remain up-to-date, and assign the responsibility of oversight to someone in each team or department who is respected by others, but also detailed enough to guarantee the documents contain the necessary information. As with previous examples, let the team define and select this person themselves.

In working with a large automotive company, I was helping a department reduce their rework. Repetitive problems were occurring amongst generally the same team members, thereby creating a perception of either a lack of ability or a lack of caring. In the early stages of the project, when meeting with employees, I was asking about work procedures and interactions amongst team members, as this is the foundation of ensuring consistency and the adoption of internal best practices. Time and again, team members either weren't aware of procedures or mentioned that they didn't use the procedures as they were too difficult to understand. Making matters worse, this organization was forced to use procedures as a way to satisfy their customers, and were in turn signing off on each order that procedures were being followed. Step one, then, was to review procedures with employees who were actually doing the work, revising and updating the documents, and making sure they were written in clear English, rather than drafted to satisfy an auditor who had never worked a day in that job.

Lastly, and most importantly, open dialogue amongst employees is key to ensuring consistency. As I wrote in my first book *Operational Empowerment*, there is nothing more effective at building communication amongst a team as holding a brief morning meeting with team members, whether they are in an office environment, out on the worksite, or in the middle of a production floor. Open dialogue on a regular basis ensures that supervisors, managers, and team leaders can communicate with employees about customer feedback (internally or externally). If structured correctly, this would allow employees the chance to provide similar feedback to improve processes or efficacies. I say "structured correctly" because meetings need to be developed with 25 percent of the time dedicated to leaders discussing their agenda, and 75 percent of the time for employees to discuss their concerns, ideas, or issues. I call this the 25/75 rule for effective employee meetings. This rule, when applied correctly, guarantees consistent and dynamic sharing of internal best practices, improving productivity, and also raising the flag to any inconsistencies or irregularities.

Having developed and applied the 25/75 rule nearly 15 years ago in leading my own team, I can tell you honestly that in any instance where an employee was thinking of leaving the department, I knew well in advance. I was able to do so through observing daily their approach to their work, their team, and their role or based on the feedback of team members, who in several instances approached me asking if I recognized an issue with an employee, and suggesting something that I might want to follow up with. The rapport and trust this approach brings is powerful.

Connecting employees with the value they bring to customers isn't difficult; it just takes a different approach in how leadership interacts with their people, and in turn how people interact with each other.

Lessons from Unstoppable Organizations

Unstoppable organizations make a concerted effort to bridge employee roles, actions, and ideas with those of satisfying customer needs and providing value. In doing so, they gain more feedback and clarity on what employees are facing when interacting with customers at various levels both directly and indirectly.

8

GROWTH IS A TEAM SPORT

Great things in business are never done by one
person. They're done by a team of people.

Steve Jobs, Former CEO, Apple

We touched briefly on some means to appeal to customers in today's online world, but as the latter continues to evolve at lightning speed, with new software, Websites, apps, and tools being introduced almost daily, it bears taking some time to discuss how some of the more commonplace tools can be used to attract and appeal to your ideal customers. Reflecting back on my earlier example of Larsen and Shaw, although a manufacturer with origins that dates back to the early 1900s and operating in what most would consider a highly traditional industry, Mary Jane Bushell and her team recognized the value of introducing more modern online tools such as social media and online chat to provide more options for customers to understand and engage with them, their products, and resources. In order to introduce these tools, however, Larsen and Shaw were strategic in making sure to consider which platforms were most likely used by their existing and potential customers. In this chapter, we're going to explore exactly why being active in today's online world is important, considerations unstoppable organizations make in doing so, the approaches and methods they deploy, and most importantly, the role employees play in helping bring an organization's brand promises and commitments to life through higher sales and more revenue.

Why Informative Selling is Dead

When considering how employees can offer value to both existing and potential customers, it's not just about the experience they provide, but also how they can entice customers through their knowledge of the product or service, and how they share this knowledge in a way that can be enticing or appealing. There are two assumptions that unstoppable organizations make that differ from what most organizations and their leadership are focusing on today; namely, that every employee in the organization is involved in sales and marketing to some extent, and that to be effective in this role, every employee must fully understand not only the value of the product or service, but how they can influence a customer's decision to buy or remain loyal. This goes beyond our previous discussions on why connecting an employee and their role with the value they offer to customers is important, and ensures that every employee is versed in how they influence the buying decisions and loyalty of existing customers. Let me share two contrasting examples to demonstrate this point.

A couple of years ago my wife and I decided to move. We contacted our intranet and telephone provider in order to have our services moved. I contacted our provider approximately six weeks before our move date to request the transfer. After waiting on hold for nearly 10 minutes, I had the opportunity to speak to a customer service agent to arrange for the transfer. It took another five minutes to provide information to verify to the agent I was in fact who I said I was, following which I explained our upcoming move and my desire to arrange for the move date. The agent replied, "I'm sorry sir, but our new software doesn't allow us to book moves so far in advance. If you can call back two weeks before your move, our new process will ensure you have a dedicated liaison to assist you with the move, and we can schedule everything at that time." After challenging this approach and the likelihood of something going wrong, I was reassured this new process was pain-free and would meet my needs. Having no further options, I hung up and rescheduled to make a second call two weeks prior to our move. The call in its entirety took about 25 minutes.

Two weeks prior to our move, I contacted the provider again, spending virtually the identical amount of time on the phone on hold, re-explaining my situation. I was transferred to a "specialist" who took down my information and reassured me we were good to go. Twenty-five minutes later, I hung up satisfied that everything was set. Unfortunately, the day before our move I was contacted by the provider's scheduling department who left a message advising that the installer for our area was ill and unable to perform the installation on the scheduled day (Friday), and would return on Monday at 9 a.m. to complete it. This would have been fine if not for the fact that:

1. We had no intention of spending the weekend without Internet and phone.
2. The new program "guaranteed" installation on the date organized, as long as notice was given two weeks prior to moving, which we had done.
3. Neither my wife nor I were going to be home Monday at 9 a.m. to meet the installer.

As I'm sure you can imagine, at this point my wife and I were quite perturbed. I attempted to contact my designated "liaison" four separate times, leaving a message three of those times during the next 48 hours with no response and no return call. On Monday, my wife rearranged her schedule, as did I, to meet the installer, who upon his arrival and hearing our story suggested that the installer in the area was not in fact sick, as it was he. He told us that the scheduling department, seeing that we were the only installation in our area on Friday, changed his schedule and moved him elsewhere for the day, choosing to wait until Monday when there were other installations scheduled near our area. All of the commitments made were changed on account of more efficient scheduling. In effect, the scheduling department misled us because of their obligation to schedule installers in the most efficient means possible.

When you break this entire situation down, there are some clear gaps.

1. The marketing department who were pushing the new "dedicated liaison" approach had failed to mention in their advertising that the "contact us two weeks prior to your move" was not optional, but now a necessity because of the software functionality used by the customer service agents.

2. Whoever had purchased and set up the software used by the customer service agents had either selected a solution that did not provide agents with flexibility to override the scheduling for customer convenience, or had not properly trained customer service agents to ensure they were notified of such functionality.

3. Customer service agents, known in this situation as "liaisons," had apparently never been told that they were to promptly return all customer calls. Two years later, I'm still waiting on Samantha to return my call.

4. The scheduling department, clearly pushed and rewarded to ensure efficient scheduling of installers, were completely disconnected with the promises being made by both marketing and the customer service agents (or liaisons).

5. The installer was also unaware of the marketing campaign and the promises made, and had not been coached on how to respond to customers in the event the intended system broke down. We appreciated his honesty, but the light he shed on the truth only served to build our resentment for the service provider.

This is a perfect example of a clear breakdown in communication between departments. The employees and their respective departments in this instance were either unaware of or completely oblivious to how their roles work together to support the customer. Each person I spoke with personally was quite friendly and attempted to be helpful, but was not clearly aware of how their actions and words influenced the value my wife and I received, or didn't receive. A few questions, then, remain for us to consider when it comes to avoiding such a catastrophe in your organization, namely:

1. How does this type of disconnect, between a well-strategized marketing campaign and the actual execution of the strategy, happen? What are the contributing factors?

2. Why in this instance were so many employees in different departments seemingly oblivious to how the program was supposed to operate, at least according to what was outlined in the marketing materials?

3. What is the severity of this incident specific to how it may have influenced existing and potential customers in their decisions to either buy from or remain loyal to this provider?

In a day and age in which customers have easy access to information about your products and services through the click of a button, a failure such as the one to deliver on a customer's expectations can be devastating. As we discussed in earlier chapters, in an age where information is easily accessible, our expectations relative to what we value have grown, as has our ability to contrast what we expected to receive versus what we actually received. Consider that 15 or 20 years ago, had this provider created a similar program, the only way we might have known about it is through a written flier, likely double-paged, which contained a few details about the program and then some other promotional material. The only way to validate this information was to call a customer service agent and talk about what we had read. Today, I can go online to obtain the same information, but typically in much more detail. With this additional information, I could also visit social media pages to validate the offer, as well as review comments and Google reviews, and within a few short minutes I could see what the company's competitors were doing in contrast.

Informative selling—telling customers what is valuable about a product or service—is dead as customers can access this information today by themselves in various formats. Instead, the key influence on an organization's ability to sustain and grow its revenue and customer base is to ensure that information shared online and through various marketing campaigns and programs is:

Relevant—built in the field with the employees who are serving customers. They know what customers want and need, and more importantly, understand what they are capable of delivering within the constraints of existing systems, processes, and time.

Clear—language should make sense to both customers and employees, avoiding legalese and overcomplicated words. I call this the "slap you upside the head with a wet fish" approach. You should know and understand when it happens.

Aligned—marketing messages shared across different marketing materials and between different marketing platforms must align with one another, with zero variance. In addition, the information that is portrayed must directly reflect what was discussed and shared by employees. Any inconsistencies only serve to confuse both customers and employees, reducing trust of the source and leading to mistakes and misinterpretations.

Not following these three golden rules of providing information that is relevant, clear, and aligned, in an age where anyone can go online and virtually kill a company's brand within minutes if their experience is not what they expected, is too risky. Refer back to my earlier mention of United Airlines ruining Dave Carroll's guitar, resulting in Dave writing a song and creating a video about the situation that has well over 15 million hits as I write this.[1]

Not doing what you say you are going to do not only detracts from value, it creates doubts about the authenticity of your organization, its products or services, and the people who work within it; worse yet, is committing something to customers that you are unable to reasonably deliver through your employees (or for which your employees fail to understand how they can deliver). Your employees are your conduits to your customers; they interpret what you say you will do, and in turn explain and act upon their interpretation with your customers. If there is lack of clarity, alignment, or realism for your employees, then revenue will diminish as a result.

Why Every Employee is in Sales and Marketing

Because customers today are so "connected," it has never been more important than now to ensure that marketing campaigns are "realistic." Making promises that can't be consistently delivered, or that haven't been identified as possible through your employees, is simply a recipe for disaster. Unstoppable organizations such as Blommer Chocolate of Canada realize that developing and successfully delivering on commitments, be they to customers, shareholders, or even a parent company begins with employees. Doug Harper is the general manager of Blommer Chocolate. In Doug's journey with his team in building a highly engaged workforce, he has ensured each year that goals and objectives that are developed by the leadership team are cascaded downward with a significant amount of input and ideas from employees in terms of the goals and how they plan to accomplish them. During our interview, Doug shared that being a small chocolate factory (there's a book in there somewhere—*Doug and the Chocolate Factory?*) the name of the game is consistently high quality chocolate in volumes that meet the committed targets. With goals and targets set, Doug and his leadership team ensure that employees are empowered as self-directed units to work together on problem-solving team challenges that in turn support improving daily operations. The combination of employee involvement in the planning for and execution of goals, along with the empowered teams, not only builds higher levels of employee engagement, but has also ensured that every goal was successfully achieved in the most recent fiscal year.

Doug's approach makes sense when setting corporate objectives. But what about connecting employees with helping the organization deliver on the claims and promises made in marketing materials and sales campaigns? This is where involving employees at all levels of the organization, more so than just those in sales and marketing departments, can guarantee that marketing materials, campaigns, and brand strategies consist of specific points of value that are not only appealing to customers, but also reasonably achievable by employees. In circumstances where I have helped CEOs and executives build their marketing and sales campaigns, we have commenced with employees from across the organization along with ideal customers, working closely with marketing and sales in order to assess and develop campaigns, programs, and promotions that fully describe an organization's goods or services. This approach involving customers occurs in four specific stages, namely:

1. Soliciting customer feedback and information.
2. Soliciting employee feedback and information.
3. Connecting feedback (from both customer and employee) with the value proposition and brand promises made by the organization.
4. Collaborative design of supporting marketing and selling materials and approaches.

In stage 1, customer feedback can be collected in various ways, including:

- Direct contact customer interviews, best completed face-to-face or, if not possible, by telephone, with questions related to the value of the product or service and their experience.
- Customer surveys, typically done electronically and presented in the first three months of the customer's experience, with questions related to understanding the value of the product or service to the customer.
- A customer advisory board consisting of a handful of long-standing customers who hold a trusted relationship and will provide feedback that is both forthright and honest relative to the pros and cons of the product or service, its quality, effectiveness, and ability to satisfy the original value commitment.
- Customer testimonials, gathered as part of the process of customer attraction and retention, at various times in the product or service life cycle, the information which can be used to further assess the points of value sought and derived by customers in different companies and segments.

In stage 2, employee feedback is collected in various ways, including:

- Employee interviews, best done in person, to understand the gaps in perception between what customers expect to receive and what they actually receive.
- Employee feedback methods such as a feedback form process on the production floor where employees fill out forms and submit them for review by a peer group.
- Employee idea boards, sometimes called "imagine" boards. Employees are encouraged to write down any and all ideas related to providing customers with a better experience or more value with the existing products or services.
- Offering specific areas on a company-wide intranet where employees can input their ideas to be shared with others and assessed by a group of peers is also a best practice.
- Focus groups consisting of a cross-section of employees from different work areas focused on a specific product or service

and how to fully describe and define the value the product or service can provide.

In stage 3, all of the input gathered is connected with the value or brand promised. This is most effectively done by creating a team that combines a cross-section of employees from various departments, along with those from marketing and sales who come together to review feedback and assess how it can be applied to create relevant and valuable marketing materials. During these sessions, the guidelines for the team to ensure they reach a consensus and the best possible outcome include:

- Disagreement on the meaning of feedback collected is to be addressed directly with the individual(s) who provided it, rather than any assumptions being drawn.
- Feedback is to be "bucketed" into categories by the team, creating value streams that can be used for different segments of customers or different applications of the product or service. For example, the feedback about the value of the large size of a new car might be best used to appeal to older generations who seek more room for comfort, as well as young families who need to carry around more toys and other ancillary items for their children. The feedback may have come from a single source, but if categorized and divided, it can provide insights into the value received by different segments of customers.
- The team is not to assess feedback against existing materials, but instead develop new materials, slogans, and information pertaining to the product or service. Starting with existing materials can sway opinions and decisions as to what feedback is relevant and what isn't. In this process, we want the group to start from what they have and what they know to be true, not what has been defined by others in the past.
- Ideas that result from the collaboration between employees and marketing and sales are to be tested with other employees and customers before ever being defined. This field-testing ensures that groupthink does not result in inadequate information.

With ideas fleshed out and further validated, the final stage is creating marketing and selling materials that use the new found information. Unlike the previous stages, employees take a back seat to the expertise of marketing, allowing them to update or create marketing vehicles that will reach the intended audience. Although employees are comfortable and acquainted with the value the products or services will bring to customers, in reality they are not necessarily the experts in how to reach the customers, although they will often have valuable input. In this situation, let marketing draw upon their expertise of how to reach existing and potential customers, and share these avenues and ideas with the teams in order to obtain feedback and further ideas. Although it may appear there is a risk that marketing will ignore feedback that may downplay or completely dismiss the ideas they create, that is not the case. In reality, by following the previous stages, a collaborative union amongst team members will have evolved—one in which employees have formed trusted relationships and can share and accept openly feedback from others. The risk that marketing will run off with some harebrained idea is unlikely if not impossible at this stage.

For a printable version of this exercise, visit *www.unstoppable organization.com*.

It was only a year ago now that I did some work with a service-based organization following the approach above. We formed a collaborative group of nearly 15 employees from marketing, sales, accounting, customer service, event planning, and operations to collect feedback from customers (both existing and potential) as well as employees on the value the organization provided. This feedback, collected through stages 1 and 2 of the process, was then reviewed and discussed relative to new marketing and selling strategies. These discussions fueled revisions to existing marketing materials and selling approaches with customers, as well as arming employees with greater information, which allowed them to become more effective at servicing their customers and providing value. Aside from creating new materials, updated content, and descriptions on their Website, some examples of how feedback influenced employees in supporting marketing and selling were as follows:

- Accounting began engaging with customers when contacting them regarding outstanding payments, using a scripted approach to best understand the value customers perceived from the service, and how receivables might ease their payment burden through options such as discounted terms, and alternate payment options such as approved credit.

- Operations began to partner with sales in attending prospective customer meetings, bridging the gap between what sales wanted to promise and what operations could reasonably deliver. In this instance, pricing quoted for customers became more closely in-line with costs as operations and sales collaborated on the quoting process.

- Customer service began attending customer meetings with sales, reducing the risk of their being placed in the "middleman" position and becoming more acquainted with the various contacts within the organization, assisting them in being more effective.

- Event planning changed their approach from signing up sponsors in preconference to doing so during conference meetings, committing to engage with sponsors who attended shows, seeking to build stronger face-to-face relationships and, in turn, signing sponsors who were happy with attendance and traffic for future events on the spot.

These are only a few of the examples that resulted from employees participating in this process. The list of ideas and actions that came from this collaborative approach to forming marketing and selling strategies was astounding. Further, employees and customers became a significant component of the marketing and selling process, ensuring that the information and content presented to customers was relevant, clear, and aligned with what was possible. More importantly, as the process progressed, all employees of the organization became more in tune with what and how they offered value to the customer, becoming in essence an informal component of the marketing and selling teams.

Creating Your Marketing and Selling Machine

Engaging employees and customers in developing marketing and selling materials, which in turn feeds marketing and selling activities, isn't new;

but in my experience, it's rare. Unstoppable organizations recognize that to have employees work in isolation is detrimental to their growth. If every employee is only an expert in their role or department, then it usually results in viewing their role, or at least that of their department, as the most important in the organization. In reality, all roles are necessary if an organization is to provide value to its customers. There's a story I read that outlines this premise. During a tour of NASA many years ago, a man was mopping the floor near the offices, strategically placing "Slippery When Wet" signs as he mopped. When the man was asked how his role contributed to putting a man on the moon, he said without hesitation, "My job is to reduce lost time accidents by ensuring the floor is slip free and people are aware of hazards." Though the truth of that story may be dubious, the message is clear. This is a far cry from someone who might respond with, "I'm just the caretaker here." As we've discussed repeatedly, when we make an effort to involve employees in the growth of our organization, we create not only a more engaged employee, but also indirectly benefit through developing an additional marketing and selling resource someone who is committed to ensuring existing customers are satisfied, and potential customers are aware of why they should engage their company. Your people, in effect, are your extended sales and marketing team if you provide them the information and knowledge.

I'm the first to admit that it is unlikely someone in accounting will want to hit the road and begin taking potential customers out for lunch. However, when your employees truly understand their role is to influence customers to repeatedly buy your products or services, the results, at least from a growth and revenue standpoint, can be powerful.

Our local Nissan dealer is a great example of this. After several years of having a manager oversee the service department, Shawn Ringel decided to shift the dealership's focus to directly supporting the advisors who were in fact the key to creating a more positive customer experience. He reconfigured the service team, removing the service manager role and instead investing in adding a service advisor to the team. He stepped in temporarily to work directly with team members and the entire service department to make sure they had everything they needed to provide the best possible environment for customers. After meeting with each of the service technicians, the service advisors, and several longstanding and forthright customers about their experience, Shawn began working with the advisors to introduce changes that were identified during the interviews. New screens were installed at the back of the service counter, allowing customers to clearly see all pricing and service options; new methods for service technicians to report their time on jobs were introduced, a direct result of recommendations made by the technicians. And of course, Shawn spent time with the advisors introducing them to various reports and data that had only previously been accessed and used by the service manager. By eliminating a layer of management and engaging both with employees and customers, Shawn was able to collaborate with his team to create an environment in which customer satisfaction (and in turn customer sales) increased. As he says, "The improvements were not my ideas; I only acted as the conduit between our great employees and fantastic customers. My role was to ensure there were no barriers to improving our customer's experience, and as a result, our employees are more focused on satisfying our customers than ever before."

This is a powerful example, but I realize that you might doubt the power or ability to introduce this approach because your business focus is selling direct to other businesses (B2B) versus consumers (B2C). Let me reassure you that the process is the same, as are the results. I can share with you an example of a large distributor, whom I worked with just over a year ago. When I met the division president, we discussed their challenges related to growth, which he summarized like this: "Shawn, if I could get my sales people to think like service, and my service people to think like sales, I'd be all set." The key issue impacting growth, he explained, was that sales often misquoted jobs, forcing service to spend additional time on jobs, often consuming additional materials. Knowing this inconsistency was not the customer's fault, costs were generally not passed along to the customer and, therefore, a substantially high number of jobs were in fact underquoted. The company was losing money.

Following the stages set forth earlier in this chapter, I began interviewing several customers to obtain their feedback on the company, its products (hoses), installation, and repair services, as well as perceptions of employees that the customers contacted. There was a clear trend. Customers experienced what the division president had referred to, as sales and service would often complain about each other while in the presence of customers. For example, if sales quoted a job, service would complain about sales and their inability to quote when arriving to install the hoses.

In turn, if service did a repair and made recommendations on replacement of hoses, sales would often push back and tell customers, "Service really shouldn't be trying to sell to you." I then interviewed employees from the sales, service, and customer service areas of the business to understand how we could further improve the customer's experience. Feedback from each of sales and service was that the other group didn't understand how to properly quote work; feedback from customer service was that they were often the referee between sales, service, and the customer, placing them in a very uncomfortable position. The three departments clearly demonstrated that there was a lack of awareness amongst the organization as to the value each role played in servicing the customer. This was leading to internal disagreements and infighting that was at times severe. Morale was low and several key people shared their desire to leave the company.

Armed with this information, I returned to the division president with a simple suggestion: create a quoting team that consisted of someone in sales and someone in service. For every new customer account, sales would always take someone from service with them when doing any quoting. For anyone in service already onsite who identifies an additional need, they would revisit the customer site with sales to further assess the situation.

Following the practices we outlined in Chapter 6 and 7, we spent time with employees in sales, service, and customer service, sharing with them customer feedback and helping each employee understand how their role contributed to the customer's experience. In addition, we spent time with the teams brainstorming ideas on how to further increase the value customers were experiencing. As you might imagine, the results were astounding. Through some collaborative discussions came several recommendations on how each role could work more collaboratively, resulting ultimately in customer quote values increasing, while time on customer installations was reduced. Customer complaints about defects or incomplete service diminished, and overall customer satisfaction improved. Most importantly, through these exercises the organization realized additional selling and service opportunities that led to higher revenues. By creating a more collaborative team of employees focused on adding value to the customer, sales and revenue grew. As you might also imagine, this collaborative approach resulted in improved morale as infighting amongst employees was reduced dramatically.

Creating a marketing and selling machine isn't about putting more people in the marketing or sales department, but instead is about helping employees understand how they do and can influence customers, and involving them in connecting their capabilities with the value customers seek.

Lessons from Unstoppable Organizations

The leaders of unstoppable organizations recognize that all employees are involved in marketing and selling, both directly and indirectly, to their customers. As a result, they focus on strategies to help their employees make this connection themselves, and then support them with information, education, and tools that will ensure they provide an exceptional experience for every customer.

PART 3 HOW TO EMPOWER YOUR ORGANIZATION TO GROW

We've spent the first two parts of this book discussing and dispelling many of the myths we've come to believe are true when it comes to growing an organization. More importantly, we've introduced various means and methods that many unstoppable organizations have used in order to create stronger connections with their employees, customers, and between employees and customers, with the latter being the most powerful. In Part 3 we will explore in greater detail how some organizations are still managing to achieve consistent levels of explosive growth, and the strategies and tactics they are deploying that have set them apart from their competition. We'll look at some examples of unstoppable organizations that are experiencing explosive growth in their market through the use of these strategies, including Hillberg and Berk, Saje Natural Wellness, and others.

9

EMPOWERING YOUR CUSTOMERS

By now you are likely either extremely excited about the opportunities that exist for your organization or you are thoroughly depressed about the fact that so many things that you once believed to be true about growing an organization are either no longer relevant or simply ineffective in today's marketplace and it's hard to clearly identify where to start. Regardless of your thoughts at this point, my goal in the next few chapters is to walk you through exactly how to shift from where your organization is today in its journey toward (or away from!) growth, to where you would like to be, providing you with a clear road map. We are going to dissect some of the minutest details of how several of the unstoppable organizations that I've introduced thus far have made this transition themselves, as well as introduce further similar organizations and discuss how they have progressed through their journey. This will help you avoid some of their mistakes and take the fastest route possible to becoming unstoppable.

Satisfying Your Customer's Perceptions

Customer empowerment is about satisfying the evolving needs of your customers, providing various incentives and a plethora of value that, in turn, influences your customer's perceptions about why they should do business with your organization. The strategies and means by which you empower your customers ultimately depend on their needs as we discussed in earlier chapters, as well as relying heavily on creating a sense of personalization for each individual customer. There should be a perception, for example, that you are providing an experience that aligns directly with what your customers need even though they may not be aware they need it yet, while ensuring a distinct, competitive advantage that results in increased revenues and supports ongoing customer loyalty. Before we delve deeper into how to make this happen, let's consider a few examples.

Amazon, a longtime and well known leader in the online marketplace, has recently been promoting their Prime membership, a low cost annual membership fee that customers can select that offers them free shipping, free two-day delivery, the ability to share the membership with up to four other people at the same address, and more.[1] For Amazon, offering an annual membership fee is alluring because it provides additional and predictable annual revenue that more often than not outweigh the actual costs of administering the membership. However, it also incentivizes customers who join Amazon Prime into using their membership more frequently to ensure they "get value for their membership." Amazon's customers weren't initially screaming for a membership option, nor were any of Amazon's competition providing something similar. However, by packaging various services and benefits together, Amazon provided a method that empowered their segment of customers who were in fact seeking more cost effective ways to reduce shipping costs and consistently receive goods much more quickly. Clearly, Amazon has done its research to make sure it is on the positive cash flow end of collecting the membership fee. In situations where they haven't been, increases to the fee have resulted. The membership fee that Amazon instituted was a direct result of providing their customers options that would, in turn, make buying from them a more valuable experience than their competition, while providing Amazon with a slow and steady form of additional revenue.

Another example of empowering the customer comes from McKenna Distribution, a family-owned business run by Steve McKenna. A distributor of flooring and flooring supplies, Steve and his team have long been conscious of what their customers, a combination of flooring contractors and retail stores, are seeking. What they have found consistently is that both of their customer segments have asked for unique products that improve their end user's experience while making the job of the retailer or contractor easier, be it in installation, competitive pricing, product quality, and so on. Steve has traveled across North America attending trade shows and connecting with manufacturers of products that suit these needs on a regular basis. This search has resulted in McKenna further expanding their product and service offerings to include a new division that specializes in design, fabrication, and installation of custom granite, quartz, and marble countertops; another example includes being the sole Canadian distributor of Wedi Shower Systems[2] and the first organization in Saskatchewan to carry a unique and natural tile line shaped from marble, basalt, and limestone called Mudtile.[3] Not only have Steve, Alyssa, and their team empowered their customers with unique products that satisfy their ever evolving needs, but Steve has also ensured that his team puts on demonstration days on a regular basis that include manufacturers of their unique products, allowing both his contractor and retail customers to connect, discuss, and review their new products, how they are installed or applied, and the unique benefits they provide to end customers. Steve and the team at McKenna empower their customers by not only constantly providing multiple options in the products and services, but also by engaging directly with customers in helping them understand the products, how they are installed, and the benefits they bring.

Several years ago, I was working with a clothing manufacturer identifying methods with which they could further empower their customers. During one of the exercises, I had a group that consisted of employees from various divisions, along with executives and leaders from across the organization, identify what they believed their customers were seeking when it came to how their garments were being delivered and received. The majority of their customers were small retail stores. Once we had made note of this feedback, I asked for the phone numbers of several customers and we reached out to them directly, identifying initially during the call our desire to continue to further improve their customer experience by asking them a few quick questions about their experience with the garments. After several calls, three distinct points arose for improvement:

1. Numerous labels on the boxes, used both for internal identification and shipping purposes, caused customers confusion and forced many of them to remove and re-label products for their own needs.
2. Bags in which garments were individually wrapped to protect from dirt and dust were unnecessary, as every customer we spoke with cleaned and pressed garments upon their receipt.
3. Efforts to expedite garments for next day delivery were unnecessary, as all customers we spoke with were expecting a "rush delivery" to take up to three days in total.

In my experience, it is rare that anyone in the organization is 100 percent clear on what customers desire from its products or services, with the exception of those actually involved in the delivery of such, because it's at this point that your customers provide their first impressions, and the individual involved in the delivery can speak to their feedback. By connecting the broader organization (including employees, leaders, and executives) with your end customers and focusing on how you can improve their experience with your products or services, organizations can in turn identify what improvements and changes are necessary that will further empower their customers with new and more valued solutions. Empowering customers is all about placing the power of the experience of your product and service into their hands, including their expectations, what would they like out of the experience, and how can you make it better. You'd be shocked at how many companies either don't solicit this information from their customers, rely solely on feedback from sales relative to this information (and sales are often biased as their goal is to make a sale, not get deeply entrenched in dealing with issues), or they outsource to an agency whose summaries are often dismissed as unrealistic or out of touch with what the organization is capable of. To empower your customers, there is no activity more important than soliciting feedback in person (recall my earlier rant about the lack of value electronic surveys provide) relative to what and how you can perform better.

To do this type of exercise, there are a handful of questions you'll need in order to flesh out specific information that is actually useful. Ask a customer too broad a question, for example, and you can expect to receive a broad answer. However, when you ask a pointed question and you're prepared to dig deeper based on the response you receive, you can build a treasure trove of information that can drive your marketing, product development, manufacturing, service levels, shipping, and the like. Here are the questions I typically use in client interactions, each one customized depending on the industry, products or services, and so on.

Customer Empowerment Questionnaire

1. What specifically do you like about our product(s) or service(s)? Can you give me two or three examples?
2. What could we change that would make your experience with our product(s) or service(s) better? How would you recommend we go about changing it?
3. If you were working in our company and could change anything, what would it be?

For bonus questions and other supportive materials, make sure you visit *www.unstoppableorganization.com.*

I want to point out a few things about these questions before you put them into practice. First, these questions contain multiple parts, and are both specific and broad. It would be difficult for a customer to answer only "yes" or "no" to one of these questions, and that's the point. Moreover, these questions are best if asked in person, not through an electronic survey. We want to have a dialogue with our customers to dig deep into their perceptions, rather than skim the surface. You'll also notice that there are only three questions, which may make you think that any response to them would be insufficient. Again, if you ask these questions in a one-on-one and face-to-face situation, you'll find conversations can run quite deep. My rule when using these questions is that every customer has feedback that would be valuable to know, but some are more forthright in giving it. As a result, sometimes I have to dig deeper or be patient in order to find the nuggets that can be gold when it comes to further improving an organization and its products or services in the eyes of its customers.

Another consideration to heed is don't ask these questions as if it's an interrogation, but rather present the questions and treat the discussion as a means to learn and understand how you can be of further service to your customers. Be comfortable in any silence that might arise during the interviews, as it might take some customers time to think about what they'd truly like to experience. Lastly, don't let the feedback become overwhelming. When you assess customer responses, look initially for trends and commonalities between responses which suggest that the feedback is important. With these responses prioritized, you can then, with time, dig deeper into customer responses to determine what might be relevant and valuable and what may simply be one customer's opinion. Above all, treat this information like gold because it is and always will be the very intelligence you need to ensure your product or service stand above your competition. Best of all, and often counterintuitive to what most think, your customers will appreciate you asking.

Empower Customers on Multiple Levels

Obtaining feedback and insight from your customers that drives how you design, deliver, and present your products and services is empowering to them. It ensures that what you provide and how you provide it is done in a way that aligns with their needs. When considering how to empower your customers, you need to think globally as there are three levels of a customer relationship you need to consider. For example, when you are dealing with a customer or even a prospective customer, rarely are you dealing with one person in one department within their organization. In a business-to-business scenario, if you are dealing with a purchasing agent, then you are not only attempting to empower the purchasing agent, but also their boss, their internal customer (often maintenance, projects, operations, or administration), and in some instances the executives who will make final decisions on whether your product or service will satisfy their needs. In a retail environment, on the other hand, you might be attempting to sell a product to a teenager, but it's likely their father and mother who are the ultimate decision-makers, further influenced by the availability of money in the bank or credit card. My point is this: when empowering your customers, you have to think in terms of levels, each level having different needs and different perceptions. In the following figure, I outline the three key levels of each customer relationship.

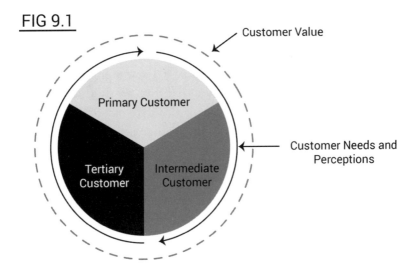

FIG 9.1

Level 1: Primary customer. This is the customer who deals directly with your staff to purchase and use your products or services. This would typically be the person who is actually using the service or taking delivery of and using the product.

Level 2: Intermediate customer. This is the customer who is influenced by and has influence over the frontline customer. Typically, he/she is the one who may not be using the product or service, but is invested in or influenced indirectly by the perceptions of the frontline customer in their experience with the product or service.

Level 3: Tertiary customer. This is the customer who is not directly or indirectly influenced by the product or service, but is influenced by the perceptions, feedback, and activities of the intermediate customer and, in some instances, the frontline customer.

What you'll notice about these three levels is that although there is a relationship, the further you move downward toward level 3, the less likely the customer will be influenced directly by the product or service. This said, historically the degree to which the product or service influences each customer level may differ, and decision-making power actually escalates as you move through the levels. For example, although the customer at level 3 may not be directly influenced by the product or service, they may make an ultimate decision on whether it is purchased which, in turn, over-rules that of the level 1 customer. Historically, customers at level 3 are known as the decision-makers or influencers.

It's for this reason that it's important to recognize there are multiple levels within your customer's organization, and that to empower your customers means you need to satisfy feedback from all three levels. This is in stark contrast to what most organizations have practiced in the past; where marketing and selling have focused on their customers, they typically focused on the tertiary or the intermediate customer, not so much the frontline customer. This is often known as "influencing the influencers," and although this strategy has worked historically, during a time when decision-making has been generally top-down with employees having little say, the times they are a-changin'.

I can recall a situation more than two decades ago now, early in my career when I was the supply chain manager for a manufacturing organization. Early one day, the company owner called me and said, "Shawn, we got a problem with our carrier, and the president of one of our largest customers wants resolution. Can you please call her to figure out what is going on?" Obviously concerned, I quickly picked up the phone and called the president of our customer to determine what was wrong. It turned out that one of the drivers of our carrier had arrived and was acting quite belligerent and rude with her shipping department, who had complained. Rather than dismiss the issue, the president had quickly called our company's president, demanding resolution or, in her words, we can consider her company to "no longer be our customer."

This was a great example of a progressive president who ensured that her employees were every bit a customer of vendors as she was. Her employees' complaints or concerns, although indirectly related to our product (the carrier was one that we had contracted with, but was not in fact associated with our company), were every bit as important as hers. This was not only an eye-opening event relative to the influence our carrier (who was not a representative of our company) could have on our customers, but also how our customers were considering feedback from all levels within their own organization when it comes to our mutual business relationship. Recognizing this, our company's president began ensuring that all sales people spent time during their visits with personnel on the floor, not just in the boardroom. Presentations began to incorporate not only the value our products could bring to our customers directly, but also how we ensured working with our company meant that all employees and customers would benefit from the relationship.

A lesson from unstoppable organizations is that influencing customers may begin at level 3 in order to become known and to hold a relationship with an influencer; however, to build a longstanding customer relationship that can grow and flourish, your organization needs to consider and support all three levels of your customers.

To fully integrate this approach to influencing customers, try this exercise with your team to gain insights on the varying perspectives that exist at each level of your customer, and more importantly, to gauge any gaps in perceptions of what each level means amongst your team:

1. How is your company today penetrating all levels of your customers' organizations?
2. To what degree do your employees recognize the various levels of influence within your customers' organizations?
3. What steps can you take to further influence your customers' perceptions through your employees? Consider marketing, sales, accounting, operations, manufacturing, shipping, and so on.

By recognizing the different levels that exist within your customer base, both existing and potential, in conjunction with clearly understanding what your customers value in your products or services, an organization is well prepared to offer value that seems so needed, necessary, and convincingly obvious from your customers' standpoint, that they will think you have created and provided your product or service just for them. This is the true formula to customer empowerment, in three separate points:

1. Continually ask your customers what they deem as valuable in your product, service, or organization.
2. Introduce this value in the form of constant improvements and changes to your products, services, or organization on an ever-escalating scale.
3. Share this increasing value with your customers, recognizing their contribution to supporting the development of such.

If empowering your customers is so simple, then why on earth isn't every organization doing it? There are a multitude of reasons this may be the case, but in my experience there is one reason that stands above all others—the perception of efficiency. That's right; all of the exercises, discussions, and interactions with customers that I've shared earlier come at a cost: time. Can you imagine creating a product and then continually asking customers how you might improve it to satisfy their needs? Sounds like a lot of work, doesn't it? Well it is, but as we've outlined earlier, it's for good reason. The problem is that all of this work can perceivably come at the cost of efficiency. How can we get good at producing one product as efficiently as possible if we are constantly improving it? How can we become efficient at taking and responding to customer calls if we are having a dialogue with many of them about how we might improve our service? The laws of efficiency in the corporate world suggest that we obtain a segment of information about our product or service, validate the information in a controlled manner, and then roll out a product or service based on that feedback, offering it at as high a price as possible while delivering it as efficiently as possible. In turn, the difference between what it costs for us to produce or deliver our product or service and what we sell it for is our profit; therefore, increasing our efficiency helps to reduce our costs and increase profits.

This is an important point, so for the sake of our further discussions I'm going to say it again. Pressures to increase efficiency and thereby increase profits come at the price of reducing the perceived value of our product and service that, in turn, reduces demand and revenue.

My point with this statement is not to suggest efficiency is a bad thing, but to suggest that in many instances our constant need to seek out further efficiencies can come at a price. More importantly, although efficiencies in our processes in how we produce or deliver a product or service may not directly influence our customer or their perceptions, there is a fine line that we need to be aware of.

Hurting Your Customer Relationships by De-Personalizing Them

If we operate from the premise that creating a perception of value for customers necessitates creating a perception of personalization to some degree for each customer, then it goes without saying that when our desire to increase efficiency crosses the line of influencing a customer's perception of personalization, we detract from perceptions of value. Put another way, counter to providing an experience in which customers have the perception that what they are receiving is of value, and to a degree to which they simply can't find anywhere else, customers in turn have an experience that suggests moving their business anywhere else would be a good idea. I call this de-personalization, and there are examples of it everywhere. Here are just a few and, for the sake of our discussion, I'd like you to consider the first thought that pops into your head when you reflect on these situations:

You place a call to a customer service desk for assistance only to be placed on hold for more than five minutes while listening to a message that says, "Our wait times are longer than expected, please be patient."

You drop by the DMV to update your license sticker, only to find a long lineup and a lack of sympathy when you reach the teller.

You stop by a bank late in the afternoon to complete a transaction that you aren't able to complete online, only to find they closed 15 minutes ago.

You buy some product that is meant to make your life easier (think of appliances, tools), only to find it breaks after a handful of uses.

You opt to pay extra for undercoating and wax sealant on your new car, only to later realize that the undercarriage is still rusting and the paint sheen (that was to last the life of your car) is now gone.

In every one of these situations, an organization, or more specifically the leadership within it, made a decision to produce or deliver a product or service in the most efficient manner at the cost of detracting from the customer's perception of value.

Why can't they hire more call center agents to take calls faster and reduce wait times?

Why don't they hire someone else at the DMV who seems to actually care about their customer's time?

Why couldn't the bank stay open later, just like every other organization?

Why did the packaging for the tool or appliance look so appealing, only to find literal junk inside?

Why didn't the dealership offer a reseal or recoat to your car in order to sustain their promise of longevity?

The answer of course is that each of these changes would cost money. What unstoppable organizations realize, however, is that being efficient can come at a hefty price when it influences a customer's perception of value, and that price is the loss of a customer's business. When we invest time in understanding, assessing, and adding value to our customers, we position ourselves, our organizations, and our people at a unique competitive advantage, which allows us to charge more, gain more referrals, keep our customers longer, and have more repeat business. All of these influence the bottom line more than efficiency ever could.

I recall one such instance in which I was attempting to return an Internet modem, having had problems with connectivity for days. Upon making several troubleshooting calls to the Internet provider, I was advised to take the modem to a nearby retail store to exchange it, at no charge. As I required Internet connectivity the next morning in order to deliver an online presentation, I raced to my local retailer to make the exchange, nervous that it may not completely resolve the issue and conscious of the fact that as we approached 5 p.m. I may be running out of options.

Upon arriving at the store, I asked the young woman working in customer service if they exchanged modems, and she replied yes. After quickly explaining my problem, I slapped down the supposedly defective modem and asked for a new one. After a curious look, the attendant looked up at me and said, "Sir, I can't exchange this." Almost immediately furious, I asked why. She responded, "You've brought me a phone modem, not an Internet modem." Realizing that, in my haste to make it to the store before closing, I accidentally grabbed the wrong modem, I pleaded for the exchange, even offering to provide my credit card to purchase the new modem. However, the young woman refused. "Our store policy states we can only exchange like for like. Now if you'll excuse me, I need to tend to the next customer," she said. Angry, I asked to speak to her supervisor, who was unavailable. After a few tense moments and recognizing that the closer we came to 5 p.m., closing time for the retailer, the fewer my chances of actually resolving the issue before morning, I left. I returned to my car where I called the Internet provider, asking them to step in and resolve the issue. After placing me on hold for several minutes and presumably speaking with their supervisor, she returned to confirm that they could not provide me with any assistance.

I share this story for a couple of reasons. First, I'm still fuming at how a situation that was seemingly simple to resolve, wasn't. If I came into a store you owned and made this same mistake, offering my credit card to pay for the modem outright, would you not take me up on my offer? Second, even escalating the situation had no influence on the outcome, which suggests that there was a lack of knowledge at virtually all levels of the organization as to what customers valued (their time, ease of accessibility to their services). My needs and, specifically, the very things that I valued as a customer were completely and utterly invisible to the eyes of these employees on account of their need (presumably as a result of management objectives and training) to be efficient and follow process, rather than service their customers.

This example demonstrates something that unstoppable organizations are aware of and, more importantly, practice almost religiously. The CEOs, executives, and employees of unstoppable organizations don't just talk, they walk their talk by putting customers first, empowering them to obtain value in the products, services, and experiences they have. If you understand how important this statement is, it will then identify how employees should not be rewarded for being efficient if achieving such detracts from the value customers receive. Unstoppable organizations place value over efficiency. I mentioned earlier the story of Zappos, initially launched as an online shoe retailer. The model of the company then and still today is that employees are encouraged to do "whatever it takes" to guarantee customers are satisfied. Company policies such as no time duration for returns and unlimited budgets for employees to make sure customers are satisfied (there are even stories of some employees actually sending flowers to customers for no apparent reason) ensure that customer value precedes efficiency.[4] The Ritz Carlton is another example of this approach at play, guaranteeing that all employees have a budget of up to $2,000 that they can spend, no questions asked, if it means the difference in satisfying the hotel patrons.[5]

Lessons from Unstoppable Organizations

Unstoppable organizations empower their customers by involving them in the process of identifying and introducing new products or services that support their evolving needs and desires. They make sure every employee supports empowering the customer by focusing primarily on adding value to every customer's experience rather than ensuring every employee is efficient.

10

EMPOWERING EMPLOYEES: THE CUSTOMER-EMPLOYEE CONNECTION

Businesses often forget about the culture and
ultimately they suffer for it, because they cannot
deliver good service from unhappy employees.

Tony Hsieh, Zappos

In the previous chapter we discussed various methods to empower our customers by collecting and (more importantly) acting on information and feedback that our employees collect from our customers on a regular basis. Recognizing that our employees are rich sources of information and customer intelligence that can inevitably help us create and provide an ongoing valuable experience for our customers isn't novel, but it certainly seems to have slipped through the cracks for many organizations and their leadership, often falling by the wayside amongst efforts to increase efficiency and streamline internal processes. There is only one source that should serve to direct what processes, policies, or technology we introduce into an organization, and that is our customer. With this in mind, we're faced with a predicament. If our efforts to improve efficiency and stream-line processes take a backseat to allowing our employees to have more personal interactions with our customers, how the heck will we ever get any work done?

Let's take a moment to review a few of the points we've discussed so far:

- Today's customers are more demanding, seeking personal-ized experiences and the perception of customization that aligns with their evolving needs.
- To reach today's customers, it's necessary to be omnipres-ent because you never know where your customers might be and what they might be reading, both in print and online.
- Responsiveness to customer needs is paramount to building and sustaining customer relationships. Keeping customers waiting for answers is no longer an option, be it in the cor-porate or retail world.
- Employees today have more education and knowledge than ever before, with an increased desire to collaborate and con-tribute in their working environment.
- The rapidly increasing size of the Millennial generation and Generation Z, with their various distinctions in needs and expectations over previous generations, will result in a shift in what our customers and employees expect in the coming months and years.
- Leaders at every level of organizations today are faced with growing pressures to deliver results, all while continually improving the morale and productivity of their employees.
- Improving the speed and consistency of employee per-formance results in efficiencies that, in some instances, detract or take away from creating a personalized customer experience.

All of these points when combined begin to shed light on the fact that the design and management of organizations today must change if we are going to survive—from how we attract talented employees, to how we retain them and ensure they are as productive and creative as possible while supporting our evolving customer needs. As we discussed in Chapter 2, what we once believed to be effective in achieving these objectives is proving to no longer be so. The hierarchal approach to leading and managing an organization, for example, with its origins dating back to the military and made popular during the Industrial Age, is simply no longer effective for attracting or engaging today's younger workforce.

The question that remains then is, if the structure we've built our organizations on is no longer relevant or effective for today's generations, what is? This isn't a simple question, and it deserves some careful consideration as we attempt to understand how to connect where we are today (a question which is built on what we've known historically to be true) to where we need to be tomorrow (a question that suggests we need to venture into the unknown, making decisions and taking actions in reformulating our organizational structures that are yet proven to be effective). Before addressing this question, however, let's address a much simpler one. Why should an organization, its leadership team, board, or employees want to introduce or support a change within their organization when nobody knows if it will even work? In other words, if the design and structure of your organization seems to be holding its own, where employees aren't leaving in droves and customers are generally stable, why fix what isn't broken? To answer this question, we need to dig deeper into understanding our employees.

Why Your Employees Might Seem Like They Don't Care

Before we answer the question I just posed, we should back up a bit. Perhaps you've attempted to introduce improvements or changes with your organizational structure or communication with the intention of making it more amenable to employees, only to find that your efforts have fallen upon deaf ears or disinterest. In my experience, when attempting to introduce changes to improve employee engagement, morale, productivity, creativity, or involvement, there are typically several common approaches most organizations take:

1. They invest in an engagement survey with employees to identify what the latter seek from their employer, their boss, and their role.
2. They invest in training leaders throughout the organization to improve their coaching and feedback skills with employees.
3. They communicate through quarterly or periodic employee information meetings in which the CEO or senior leaders speak to employees about the state of the business.
4. They introduce a new means of recognizing employee performance tied to providing monetary rewards through different means.

When you first look at this list, you'll notice some themes amongst these various initiatives. First, they are often introduced *to employees*, rather than a result of employee feedback or requests. Second, they require a change in employee behaviors or actions initially in order to be successful. Third, and most importantly, they are only successful or effective if employees buy into the fact that there are advantages they might personally experience from following along and supporting such initiatives.

For example, what are the tangible benefits that leaders will receive from taking training? Will it make their days shorter or their interactions with employees easier?

What are the advantages your employees will receive from participating openly and honestly in an engagement survey? Will all of their concerns be addressed? Will they receive the improvements they are seeking in their roles or working environment?

How do the employee information meetings serve to help employees? Will this newfound information make their jobs easier or provide them with more autonomy to make decisions?

If the initiatives you undertake to improve employee morale, engagement, and involvement are perceived as not being helpful to employees, then they will fail, plain and simple. The very introduction of these initiatives often misses the boat in employees' eyes because they fail to address the most important question in the mind of every employee: "What's in it for me?"

Let's drill down a bit further and consider for a moment the infamous "employee engagement survey." Typically, this is a series of questions asked of employees in an electronic format, providing feedback based on employee selection of predetermined options on topics related to culture, leadership, compensation, and the like. If you or your organization has ever undergone an employee engagement survey, you'll know that the amount of information received can be daunting, a seeming fire hose of employee complaints that are often unsubstantiated and geared more toward everything an organization is doing wrong rather than right.

Other than the ineffectiveness an electronic version of this type of survey can present (which we discussed in earlier chapters), there is a glaringly obvious problem with employee engagement surveys that appears to be not so obvious. Consider a survey you've taken personally in the past; possibly it was an online survey for a retailer such as Home Depot, or a survey sent to you after you purchased a product online. What was it that drove you to invest your own personal time and effort into answering that survey? My guess is you completed the survey when you were either ecstatic with the product or service, or you were absolutely disgusted with the same. Both positions are extreme and motivating enough to encourage you to invest time in completing the survey to communicate your emotions, good or bad. Now apply this same methodology to employee engagement surveys and you may start to recognize exactly why surveys can often be grouped into two categories: those who seem to love working for an organization versus those who seem completely disgusted with not only the organization but everything about it, including the survey itself.

This suggests that quite possibly the results we receive from engagement surveys are not as valuable as they might appear to be on the surface. In addition, a question of accuracy comes into play. If an employee has a bad day or a bad experience on the day they complete the survey, it's possible that frustrations that may normally not be so prominent will shine through in the survey results. A manager that they normally get along with might suddenly be the worst manager ever on account of a conversation they had earlier in the day. Simply put, holding engagement surveys in this manner, as a sort of test that employees have to complete, is only placing work on the employees that doesn't help them in the short-term or long-term. Moreover, most employees have had multiple experiences of completing a survey only to find that nothing, on the surface anyway, seems to improve.

Is there a better solution? Yes, and it extends beyond simple surveys. The best solution for obtaining employee input and ideas on how to improve your organization's working environment for example, including specifics on leadership, compensation, process improvement, and the like is to simply ask your employees for their feedback, one-on-one and face-to-face. No buttons to press and no submissions to be saved. This can be done individually or in focus groups, but the key is that in this format any responses and feedback can be validated, with the trained interviewer having the opportunity to judge and dig deeper based on responses, participants' body language, and various other nuances. These, in turn, help to determine what questions require further dialogue and elaboration, versus those that are simple and to the point. Say, for instance, you were to ask a question such as this on an electronic survey:

"What characteristics do you like about your direct manager?"

For participants to respond, the only options that are electronically available result from (a) pre-populating several characteristics that might drive employees to respond in a certain fashion, or (b) leave a comments box open. Rarely is option (b) taken without first providing pre-populated options, as it makes it difficult to sort responses and look for trends. The problem with this approach comes when we consider the pre-populated options. First, how do we know if the pre-populated responses may be relevant to the employees' actual desired response? Second, how do we learn what's behind the chosen option(s) that explains why an employee would feel this way? Third, what options exist to dig further, as initial responses seem only superficial in nature? The answer to all three of these questions is clear—you can't. This is why electronic employee engagement surveys (or customer surveys for that matter) are garbage. They serve no more than to put checks in boxes and allow the original respondent to say that they have in fact completed a survey.

When I have shared this idea with proponents or even sellers of employee engagement survey systems and software, I've come up against harsh criticism. The main argument they often present is that by completing a survey electronically, organizations and their executives can compare responses to that of their competitors creating a benchmarking opportunity. This may be true, but if you have to pay for the survey (and in any instance I've come across, you have to), then why would you pay for this benchmarking information when you can glean it from discussions with others in your sector? Organizations such as the Excellence in Manufacturing Consortium, for example, provide ample opportunities for their members to network and share benchmarking information as part of membership. They encourage their members to share not just benchmarking and experiences relative to employee engagement, but all areas that impact member performance such as productivity, safety, energy management, and so forth.

An electronic employee engagement survey, such as training or mandatory meetings or even new means of providing employee rewards, is often perceived by employees as "just another management initiative." You know the kind. New ideas, systems, processes, or technology that likely require employees to do something different or in addition to their existing duties with a promise of helping to curb some undesirable features or enhance an existing "organizational performance."

When it comes to engaging our employees, we have to remember one thing. Employees only care about the organization if they can tie its success directly to their daily activities and role within and, in turn, achieve personal success as a result of supporting their organization's success.

Too many "changes" that are proposed often inevitably create more work for employees, rather than help them to better support their customers and achieve a feeling of personal satisfaction. Ultimately then, there is an employee disconnect that is further exacerbated as more "initiatives" or "changes" are introduced. It's for this very reason that many organizations that have invested heavily in completing employee engagement surveys or in training for their leaders still have employees with low levels of engagement. It's time to stop initiating changes that are for the betterment of the organization, and instead create an environment in which employees identify and initiate the changes themselves. This creates a more positive working environment, increasing productivity and morale consecutively. This is, in my definition, the premise of employee empowerment, and it is the key to creating an organization of employees who care about their customers, their work, and each other.

What is Employee Empowerment?

The best way to engage employees, hands down, is by empowering them. The concept of employee empowerment isn't new; in fact, I believe much of the term's philosophy originates from the understanding and benefits that tools such as the lean system have provided, which promote a culture of continuous improvement where employees are focused on improving how they work to best satisfy the needs of the customer.[1] Empowering employees is about realizing that they are the most knowledgeable and best suited to identify and improve how work gets done. It's about shifting the creativity and decision-making ability to the employees, allowing them the opportunity to enact changes and improvements, introducing systems that make their jobs easier, and helping them be more effective in serving the customer. The following figure outlines the framework for employee empowerment.

FIG 10.1

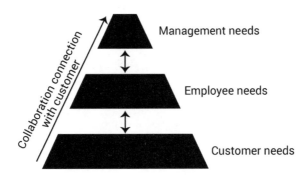

There are a plethora of proven examples of employee empowerment, one being Zappos, the online shoe retailer I referenced earlier and whose CEO, Tony Hsieh, embarked on a journey several years ago to remove literally all managers from across the organization, shifting instead to a self-managed, self-organized company structure.[2] Zappos' approach may seem a little extreme and is not always necessary, as even shifting some level of autonomy to employees can dramatically influence an organization's ability to succeed in today's marketplace. Consider the approach of Mike Vokes, discussed earlier, who shifted the decision-making ability down to his teams, moving away from a centralized leadership model.

Beyond increasing employee engagement, shifting autonomy to employees actually appeals to today's younger generations who are more comfortable with a collaborative approach to decision-making. This results in higher levels of employee retention and guarantees that decisions are made faster, which enables a more productive working environment. In addition, empowering employees is most effective at ensuring organizations become and remain profitable, given we use the following logical assumptions:

1. The majority of employees accepts and remains in their functional role with the expectation of and desire to work as effectively as possible.
2. Most employees would make decisions that are similar to those of management if provided the same information and context.
3. Employees are best suited and positioned in their roles to make sure customers are satisfied both directly and indirectly.
4. Leaders are unable to be everywhere all of the time; therefore, it makes more sense to shift the decision-making ability to employees to ensure rapid response to customer needs and effective changes in process.
5. Employees are the best positioned to identify what needs to change in order to work efficiently while still servicing the needs of customers.

The logic behind these assumptions is generally received more positively by younger generations than those who are older. This is understandable when we consider that someone who spent his entire working career being told what to do by his boss is more likely to reflect on that situation and believe it is the best approach, versus someone who may have in more recent years experienced a boss who provided freedom in making decisions and taking action, and who would believe *this* approach to be more effective. I've also found that those who are most likely to push back on the concept of employee empowerment are, not surprisingly, leaders themselves.

I completed some work with a small team of 25 employees working within a large association. Our work spanned several months, during which we shifted them from an environment in which the employees were overseen by two separate managers, to a fully empowered team with autonomy to make their own decisions and having no managers. We had commenced the work by redeploying the two managers to different roles outside the team and putting some consistent communication practices in place, including a weekly meeting with the team's director to discuss changes that were happening both at the organizational level (director's world) and the operating and customer-facing level (the employee's world). In addition to these weekly meetings, employees held a daily morning meeting in which they briefly discussed what they were working on for the day and week, and acknowledged any support or impact their work would have on others within the team. Tracking of individual work and projects was completed on a white board and updated by a team champion on a daily basis based on feedback and discussions during the morning meeting. It was these three key changes that were the basis of shifting from an environment in which two managers delegated work and made decisions, to a team environment in which employees made their own decisions.

Why did the director decide to make such an extreme shift, you might wonder? Well, team morale had been extremely low for years, productivity levels were down, and some very talented employees, who got along well with others and were productive in earlier times, had started to leave the team. The director, clearly concerned, had recognized through exit interviews that both of the managers were perceived as micromanaging team members, isolating the employees from each other and creating a somewhat toxic environment in which employees were not serving each other or their customers effectively. By shifting to a more empowered model, not only did productivity improve, but so did team morale and willingness to work with and support one another. For the purposes of helping you to make this transition, I've outlined the exact approach that we took in the following.

Six Steps to Empower Employees

The shifts to transitioning to a culture in which employees are empowered can differ depending on the existing culture, leadership style, and structure of the organization; however it follows six steps.

STEP 1: FEEDBACK

Interview employees on the team to understand what is working well and what is not working well, as it pertains to getting work done. Clearly identify any obstacles, bottlenecks, and restrictions that slow the completion of work or create conflict amongst the team.

STEP 2: PLAN

Formulate a plan to redesign the working team(s) aligned on departmental and individual objectives and skills, redeploying leaders in nonmanagement roles.

STEP 3: COMMUNICATION

Identify new methods of communication to ensure individuals within the team communicate on existing work priorities, challenges, and needed support on both a daily (morning brief) and weekly (in-depth review) meeting.

STEP 4: PLANNING

Identify the best methods to communicate work status, incorporating the use of visual tools such as white boards or smart boards, as well as online scheduling tools for more in-depth work tracking. Technology options vary widely, but should provide the information employees need in a timely manner and require little input or effort from employees to manager.

STEP 5: CHAMPIONS

Identify formal and informal team champions to support the initiatives and ensure processes are being followed. These are typically employees who have the respect of other team members and have the ability to support work scheduling and communications.

STEP 6: INTRODUCTION

Introduce the plan to existing employees to outline changes and gain further insights. In addition, introduce plans to customers both internal and external to identify improvements and to demonstrate any changes in service levels and contacts. Warning: it is during this stage that plans will receive pushback and employees may disagree with the approach. Following the stages set forth previously, and including employees throughout, will ensure this is not another management initiative. This said, the degree to which employees push back will determine the extent to which further changes need to be made, and will also support whether a smaller pilot initiative should be introduced to further prove the system and increase employee buy-in and engagement with the process.

For bonus resources and tips on how to empower your employees, make sure you visit *www.unstoppableorganization.com*.

It's important to take a moment to revisit a point I referenced earlier. Empowering employees results in higher levels of engagement. Said differently, the degree to which employees are empowered will determine the extent to which you experience improvements in engagement. Shift a few decisions to employees while leaving the existing management structure in place and you'll see marginal improvements, if any. Take a more extreme approach such as the situation of the association I shared above and you'll find significantly more improvements in both employee morale and productivity.

With this shift toward empowerment, there is another benefit that is often not considered. As it's typically management that deals with customers either internal or external, then shifting away from having many (or any) internal managers will create a closer connection between employees and customers. This may make you weary of such a change, but similar to the benefits of employee empowerment, this too will further improve the performance of your organization. I call this the customer-employee connection.

The Customer-Employee Connection

The customer-employee connection is a concept I outlined in my first book, *Operational Empowerment*, defining it as a critical component to ensuring customers have the perception of value in every transaction they have with your organization. Specifically, as your employees are connecting with your customers every day on various levels, it goes without saying that helping employees understand what your customers value, and how they can provide it, is critical for an unstoppable organization. Creating this customer-employee connection is a natural evolution of empowering your employees as, for employees to make educated decisions and in turn take actions to support your customers, they must be empowered. More succinctly, empowering employees will yield a stronger customer-employee connection.

FIG 10.2

In order to facilitate a strong and constructive connection between customers and employees, there are several considerations to take when transitioning to an empowered team or culture, namely:

1. Value of time: Customers today want their products or services delivered to them in record time, set to their specific agenda. What this means is that, in servicing customers, there is a conflict between an organization's desire to process customer needs quickly, versus the customer's needs to ensure the time spent with them satisfies their needs.

2. Product or service knowledge: Employees must be fully versed in and able to quickly access information about the product or service they are providing if they are to satisfy the customer. Returning back to point 1, if customers value time, then having employees place them on hold or not return calls only serves to annoy them.

3. Customer needs: As we discussed in earlier chapters, not only is it important for an organization to understand the evolving needs of its customers, it's also important for employees to understand the specific needs of their direct customer. Externally, this might seem simple and information can be collected and distributed based on customer interviews, but we also need to consider internal customers. Does finance understand why holding off on the next equipment purchase will be detrimental to productivity and increase the risk of missing production targets?

By empowering employees with a better understanding of both internal and external customer needs, organizations can create a stronger customer-employee connection whereby customer needs always come first.

As an example of the power of this connection, I will share my experience with an organization I worked with nearly two years ago which transitioned to an employee-empowerment model. Initially, I interviewed several employees in the organization's accounting department and when I asked them what end they believed their end customers desired, they looked at one another and guessed, "Lower prices?" Digging further, I asked where this perception had come from. Most replied that they were only presuming this was the need, as they couldn't figure out why customers would pay so much for their products considering how inefficient the organization was. Yikes! Educating employees on customer needs is critical to creating the right mindset and providing sufficient information in an environment in which employees can make their own decisions.

Lessons from Unstoppable Organizations

Unstoppable organizations empower their employees with more autonomy and authority as they recognize that doing so increases the engagement of their employees. This in turn increases their employees' desire to not only work effectively, but tirelessly in ensuring every customer has an exceptional experience.

11

EMPOWERING YOUR BRAND

A brand for a company is like a reputation for a person.
You earn reputation by trying to do hard things well.

Jeff Bezos, CEO, Amazon

With employees motivated and empowered to support customers, organizations in turn need to recognize that it's entirely possible to dramatically increase the power of your brand and through their employees. Building on points we discussed in earlier chapters, marketing is best *enabled* by employees who clearly understand and connect with customer needs. This is more than just recognizing the value that employees can bring to building brand awareness. It also understands that a growing percentage of today's customers are conscious of what organizations stand for and how they treat the environment as well as their employees. It truly is about the connection employees have with the company and the brand that sets high-growth organizations apart from others.

What's in a Brand?

When it comes to building a brand, you may initially think of global power house brands such as Coca-Cola, Apple, or Microsoft. I once heard someone explain that a brand has reached the pinnacle of success when the name of the brand actually replaces the product or service they are selling. Q-tip, Kleenex, Band-Aid, Windex, and Ski-Doo would all be examples of organizations and brands that have reached this level of success. Although I think this explanation of a brand makes sense, it creates for many organizations what can only be perceived as an unattainable goal. A slightly more realistic goal is to consider the point at which your organization's name or the name of your product or service is recognized by both existing and potential customers as the "go-to" source.

Although this definition seems quite valid, it's missing something. If we refer back to our earlier conversations, we've discussed at length the fact that an organization is built on and around its employees, and as a result, an organization's existing and potential employees must also somehow connect with its brand. Although a brand is typically something that is only customer-facing, the fact remains that unstoppable organizations recognize that a brand must appeal to not only customers, but also employees. Michael Beneteau, of CenterLine (Windsor) Limited, one of Canada's Best Managed Companies, is the CEO of an unstoppable organization who believes this to be true. When I asked Michael how he and his team have built such a highly successful organization that has more than 700 employees in multiple locations serving customers from around the world, Michael gave me a different take on what a brand is. You see, Michael connects CenterLine's brand with that of the organization's employees.

Although CenterLine's core product is that of designing and servicing custom automation, their success as an organization has come from having the right people and the right culture. Michael described CenterLine's brand as "customer first," something that has ensured the long-term growth and success of the organization. Michael and his team measure the success of their culture and their "customer first" brand by continuously asking customers what sets CenterLine apart from the competition. Repeatedly they are told that it is their people; not necessarily the skills of their people (although these are important), but rather the way in which CenterLine employees put their customers first, building strong and lasting relationships. This constant feedback confirms that CenterLine is indeed spot-on with their brand and culture.

This "customer first" approach is so critical to CenterLine's success that Michael and his team realized that the key to achieving their commitment was to create brand awareness that was embraced by not only customers, but also potential employees. When I asked Michael to describe this approach, he said, "We instill a brand awareness with young people; we want to be known amongst our potential employees as a training organization that supports young people. In doing so, we attract the best talent, which appeals to our customers and in turn helps us to live and breathe our 'customer first' commitment."

I asked Michael how well this branding with potential employees works and whether they ever experience employee turnover, to which he responded, "Our philosophy of being a training organization that supports young people means that we do lose some of our staff, but we are always sure to leave the door open." What Michael confirmed is that sometimes employees will realize that working for CenterLine isn't the right fit for them and if this is ever the case, then those employees should pursue other interests or careers. "I always let our employees know that if they decide to leave and things change, they should contact us first."

I was invigorated after speaking with Michael, as I was with others interviewed for this book. In summarizing some points gleaned from my discussion with Michael as well as several other CEOs, the best approach to building a successful brand is quite contrary to what we've historically believed to be the power of a brand. Namely, success results from:

- Having two brands: a customer-facing and an employee-facing brand.
- Their customer-facing brand of "customer first" is also their cultural focus.
- Their employee-facing brand of "A training organization for young people" also appeals to their customer base.
- The brands coexist in benefiting the organization, its customers, and stakeholders, but create a foundation and focus that places employees first.
- Both brands are clear, concise, and meaningful to anyone who comes in contact with them.

The long-term and continued success of CenterLine's approach to building a brand that is both employee-centric and customer-centric, serving to create meaning for both groups while primarily satisfying the need for employees with the right skills, mindset, and values, clarifies what a powerful brand really is and what it isn't.

Redefining What a Brand Is

When you consider the simplicity of CenterLine's approach to creating a brand, and the power and undisputed success they have had in growing their organization, their philosophy sheds new light on how unstoppable organizations are looking at their branding. Of course, CenterLine, like other organizations, invests in marketing that is relevant and meaningful to their customers. What Michael and his team have recognized, though, is that the best investment they can make to grow their organization is not in creating marketing campaigns, but in finding, attracting, and growing young talent that adopt and connect with the customer-first philosophy, because it's this philosophy that is the key differentiator for CenterLine in what is a crowded market of competition.

Using this as an example, we can reshape our definition of a brand, recognizing that even in an industry that is highly focused on technology, such as CenterLine, it's truly an organization's employees who help it differentiate and stand out in the market. By incorporating employees into the development of a brand, we empower the brand to come alive. Similarly, Michael and his team realized that in order to place "customers first," CenterLine as an organization needed to be first and foremost a training organization for young people to learn, grow, and increase their knowledge.

Michael's approach to developing a brand is not new, although it is unique in that very few CEOs see a brand as being positioned first and foremost around employees. In order to assess what aspects are most important to both your employees and customers, begin with conducting some focus groups to address questions such as the following:

1. What is it that your customers find most unique or valuable about your organization (not just its products or services) that helps you to stand apart from the competition?

2. Identify the contributors to achieving this value, both from the perspective of your customers but also from internal dialogue with employees. Specifically, what are the key contributions the organization makes that ensures it provides this value on a continuum to your customers?

3. How does the organization make these contributions? What are the sources of the contributions; how are they attracted or found; how are they sustained?

4. What are the most successful sources of these contributions today? How can these sources be further improved?

5. Where might these sources be found in the next five to 10 years? How can the organization position itself to be connecting and attracting these sources to ensure their longevity?

Working through these questions is, in my experience, an exercise best completed by individuals not engaged in marketing, selling, or any other department for that matter, as their views and experiences can ultimately influence the responses. Ideally, you should have someone neutral from your organization, an individual not presently involved directly with any department or team to interview your customers and provide this summary. I'm not suggesting you grab someone off the street per say; however, considering the various influences those from across the organization can have based on their own departmental and personal objectives, it is better to have an outside expert conduct these interviews for three reasons:

1. A customer-centric focus. An outsider is not worried about trying to justify to your customer why they may not be pleased with some aspects of your organization and satisfied with others. They simply want to collect the information as it is presented, with no existing biases or conflicting priorities.

2. Message clarity. Similar to my recommendations on avoiding electronic employee engagement surveys, by having someone hold face-to-face discussions with your customers, they have the opportunity to dig deeper when confused by or are unfamiliar with customer comments. Professionals who conduct these types of interviews know when to dig and when to rest, with the benefit to the organization being complete clarity about customer ideas, feedback, and concerns.

3. Additional value. In my experience, customers are elated at the fact that one of their suppliers or partner companies (your organization in this case) is interested in learning how they can do more and be more to and for their customers. This is indirectly a means of adding value to your customers and further entrenching your organization as vital to the success of your customers.

With this new view of what a brand really entails, and some ideas on how to identify the very components of your brand that are both appealing to customers and attractive to potential employees, let's turn the tables for a moment to explore how to empower your brand.

What's Your Brand?

Let's take a moment to develop your organization's empowered brand. Ideally, you will do this with a cross-section of people from your organization (not just senior leaders, but also managers, supervisors, and most importantly, employees along with a small collection of key suppliers and important customers). The best group size for this exercise is between 10 and 12 people. You can of course do this exercise yourself first, to see how it works, but the best results come from gaining multiple inputs from employees, customers, and key suppliers.

Consider for a moment what your organizational brand or value promise is. Write it down at the top of a piece of paper or as the header on a flip chart, and then below this statement, draw two columns. On the left, title it "customer," and on the right, title it "employees." I've created an example in the following figure.

Ignoring your value statement for a moment, under the left column, identify all of the things that customers value from your products, services, and organization. When you describe this, don't think about what goes into creating or delivering the value, but rather the value customers receive as a result. A customer would not describe your technology as something they value, but rather what they receive or achieve as a result of your technology. Apple describes its watch as helping customers to "live a better day" (the intended result of wearing it), rather than focus on the specifications or technicalities of the technology that goes into every watch.

FIG 11.1

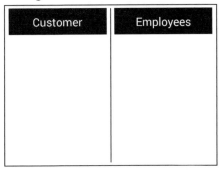

Organizations Brand Promise

Customer	Employees

Some examples to consider include:

- Quality or durability of your product.
- Responsiveness of your team (customer service, technicians, etc).
- Location or availability of your facilities.
- Attitude of your employees.
- Knowledge that your employees possess.
- The improved lifestyle or experience.

Now, under the right hand column titled "employees," describe the attributes and benefits that employees appreciate in working for your organization. Examples to consider may include:

- Support of leadership.
- Freedom to set their own schedule.
- Location of your facilities.
- The value your product or service provides customers.
- The reputation of the organization.
- The impact your products or services have on the world.

With this information documented, the next step is to identify the top three points on each side. For example, identify three points that customers value and three points that employees value. These are the foundation of your new brand. Before we go any further, if you aren't sure how to

identify the top three points in each category, use a process of prioritiza-
tion. My favorite is to have everyone involved write down on a sticky note
what their single most important top priority would be from each side,
then have them write it down and collectively share their sticky notes,
working as a team to determine what the priority would be. Invariably, in
my experience of completing this exercise through several years now, there
has never been a team that hasn't reached a collective agreement on what
the top three priorities will be, although sometimes individuals have a difficult time identifying what their single most important priority would be
for each category.

Make sure to visit *www.unstoppableorganization.com* to grab a printable
version of this exercise to assist you in developing your empowered brand.

These priorities now provide the basis for identifying your double-sided
vision; specifically a statement that encapsulates what customers value, but
also aligning this with what potential employees value. Returning back to
Michael and his team at CenterLine, their customer brand is "customer
first," and their employee brand is "We are a training organization for
young people." What these two statements suggest is that CenterLine is
seeking young people to train them in guaranteeing that their customers'
needs are always put first. How can you argue with such a strong brand
statement? More importantly, how CenterLine lives this statement is how
they empower their brand. These aren't just broad statements, but actual
benefits that the organization ensures are engrained in daily operations.

From the employee side, CenterLine gets involved in sponsoring
events and competitions by offering up their facilities and equipment to
young teenagers still in school. This creates awareness in young people
and supports their brand of training young people. On the customer side,
CenterLine places an employee with their customers for specific projects,
partnering with customers to hire talented people who are involved in the
building of the customer's automation. The intention is that the employee,
who will be on CenterLine's payroll during the build and installation, will
then transfer to becoming an employee of their customer once the installation and testing is complete. They are partnering with their customers
to ensure that their brand of "customer first" is achieved by hiring and
training employees (employee brand promise) to learn and be involved in
their customer's large automation projects such that they become a subject

matter expert for the customer, involved from the beginning to end of the build, installation, and application of the automation. In this way, they are placing their customer first in ensuring they have all of the knowledge and experience they need in-house.

This is a perfect example of an empowered brand, one which has three components that describe succinctly what customers find of greatest value in your organization, but also a complementary statement that describes what you offer to employees that is of value to them. This, in turn, is supported by continuous actions that demonstrate and support the achievement of both.

Empowering Employees Brings a Brand to Life

In Chapter 10, I discussed how unstoppable organizations empower their employees, and the multitude of benefits this provides not only for the organization, its employees, leadership, and shareholders, but also its customers, which drives higher revenue, profitability, and market share. More specifically, when you consider creating a brand that is empowered, the only means to successfully achieve and deliver the brand promise is to ensure that everyone, including your employees, is involved.

Following our discussions, then, take a moment to reflect on some of the most recognized brands that you can think of, and ask yourself the following questions:

1. Does the brand speak to both adding value to the customer and motivating and inspiring employees?
2. Does the organization empower their employees to support and satisfy the value promise?
3. How can you create a more empowered brand that will drive more value to customers while motivating employees?

Lessons from Unstoppable Organizations

A brand is not a slogan that is meant to appeal only to customers, but rather a phrase that employees and customers alike can experience in their every interaction with an organization. Achieving this multifaceted means of forming a brand ensures that unstoppable organizations attract the right talent to best support their customers.

12

EMPOWERING MARKET SHARE

> *When you improve your product so that it does the customer's job better, then you gain market share.*
> **Clayton Christensen, American scholar**

We've spent considerable time so far discussing how the most unstoppable organizations focus on empowering their customers by empowering and engaging their employees. In this chapter, we are going to explore the shortest path to not only achieve growth, but also grab market share from your competition by empowering your market share.

Adapting to Tomorrow's Customer: Thinking Forward

I define the concept of "thinking forward" as the ability to think about, focus on, and consider what's likely to change or shift in the next five to 10 years, versus what's happening now. Unstoppable organizations are always thinking forward, which in turn often means they are making shifts and changes when other organizations deem them unnecessary or even inappropriate. In this chapter, then, I'd like you to think forward in order to prepare for what's to come.

Based on our discussions and the information I've shared with you so far, let's take a few minutes now to complete a "think forward" strategy for your organization. I'll share some questions with you, and you can take some time to reflect upon them, and then jot down your ideas and responses. Similar to previous exercises, this is best completed by involving a cross-section of your organization, specifically a combination of leaders, employees, key suppliers, and customers. This of course can also be done on your own to gain some perspective before introducing any new ideas to your team.

The Think Forward Strategy

1. Think about your organization five years from now and consider what will change in the following areas:
   - Your employees: what are their skills, needs, attitudes, desires, and demographics?
   - Your customers: what are their needs, tendencies, influences, and preferences?
   - Your market: is it growing or shrinking? What does your competition look like?
   - Politics: how are local, regional, and national politics influencing your business, employees, and customers?
   - Environment: are there changes in the environment that influence your organization, its employees, customers, products, or services?
2. Think about and consider your product(s) or service(s) five years from now. How will demand have evolved (good or bad)? What will the influences on this demand shift be? What will your competition be involved in; will they be ahead of the curve or behind it?

3. Think about technology that influences your customers and employees today. How might this technology change or evolve, and how might these changes influence your customers or employees?

With your responses to these questions noted, identify a timeline that steps through each year starting with the current year and ending five years into the future. Under each year, identify four categories:

1. Product or service
2. Customer
3. Employees
4. Competition

Next, under each category place your comments and points made in the earlier questions, essentially creating from your perspective what a timeline of events might look like. Sure, this is a guess on your part, but creating this timeline is more than most ever do for identifying what may happen in the coming years, so give yourself some credit.

With the timeline completed, you now have a timed sequence of events that will allow you and your team to be clear on how your market will evolve. With this information in hand, you are now in a great place to identify the strategies and tactics necessary to combat, counteract, and adopt these evolutions in order to gain an edge on your competition, and more importantly, to ensure you and your organization aren't left behind. With this timeline created, you can now shift toward the planning stages to capitalize on any shifts in the market. To demonstrate, let's take a point from your information and build it out. Referring back to our earlier discussions, one of the points that unstoppable organizations consider is that their customers are becoming more aware, and thus expect an increased ability to customize the products or services they acquire. So let's spend a few minutes incorporating considerations of your future customers.

Capitalizing On the Next Generation

Considering the "Think Forward" exercise earlier and considering our customers, our focus should be on the predominant generation that will dominate both buying trends and employment trends in the next five to 10 years, rather than be overly concerned about which generation has these greatest influences today. Drawing upon our earlier discussions of the Millennial generation, a landmark study published in the *Journal of Personality and Social Psychology* identified this generation as the "me generation," finding that Millennials are "much more likely to value money, image, and fame than things like self-acceptance, community, and the environment."[1] The outcomes of this study provide some key insights into how an organization can position its products and services in order to appeal to the shifting needs and desires of the Millennial generation and future generations to come. It also sheds light on what changes an organization should undertake to attract the right employees—if we apply our earlier logic that employees will determine how strongly your customers connect with your organization, its products, and services. For insights into how unstoppable organizations are positioning themselves to draw upon generational preferences in a way that thinks forward, we need look no further than Rachel Mielke, CEO of Hillberg and Berk Jewelry. Ever since a brief appearance on the television show *The Dragons' Den*, Rachel and her team at Hillberg and Berk have been growing and expanding their jewelry sales and clientele around the globe. "The key to growth," says Mielke, "is in having the right culture—one that can connect with the organization's purpose. At Hillberg & Berk, all of our employees connect with our purpose, which is to inspire sparkle and empower women to live with passion and positivity."[2] When I asked Mielke how she ensures her employees connect with the organization's purpose, she said that each year the staff spends time in training that specifically focuses on helping employees connect with the organization's values—what they mean to the organization, to customers, and to every team member's role. At Hillberg and Berk, it isn't about identifying the corporate values or purpose on a plaque that resides in the boardroom or lobby, but rather helping every employee connect their role and the value they bring with creating a positive customer experience that exceeds expectations and helps clients live the very same purpose and values.

You might be wondering why Mielke and her team focus so intensely on building a culture that connects with and lives the organization's purpose, but in her eyes the reasons are quite simple. "We are aware that the workforce of today, and more importantly, that of tomorrow, is different. Organizations need to be brave in how they structure their working environment in order to appeal to, engage with, and empower employees. At Hillberg & Berk we want to provide our team with the freedom to guide how they work, where they work, and what they work on," she says.

Rachel and her team recognize how crucial it is to find and keep the best employees in order to create the best customer experience and, in turn, grow their organization by capturing new market share. Her ideas and approach are something we've heard from other CEOs and leaders in this book, such as Doug Harper, general manager of Blommer Chocolate, and Michael Beneteau at CenterLine, each overseeing an organization that is very different from one another, yet each experiencing nonstop growth, and each holding a similar philosophy for how their employees are key to their growth. What Rachel also shares in her example is the necessity to think forward about how tomorrow's customers and employees want their experience to be, specifically focusing on how to create a better online and in-store customer experience to satisfy Millennials, while also creating a working environment that is appealing to them.

Thinking forward about the kind of environment and experience the next generation might want helps to shape the ideas of how an organization needs to focus more on culture—finding first the right employee, and then fitting the role to the employee, rather than fitting the employee to the role. This, in turn, shapes an environment in which employees are engaged, motivated, and perform at their highest levels of productivity, serving customer needs and being content staying with their organization for the long-term.

Why Being Brave is Par for the Course

Taking Rachel's comments to heart, it's important to reflect on how "organizations need to be brave." Brave indeed. With the Millennial generation now being the predominant buying and employee generation combined, their needs, real or perceived, will continue to directly influence the success of any organization, often in more ways than one. CEOs like Rachel, who realize that there is a direct correlation between the culture of their organization and the ability to sell and meet evolving customer needs, are ahead of most.

It is in being brave in shaping and nurturing an organization's culture that unstoppable organizations can ensure their customers have an exceptional experience. Reflect back on our earlier example of the distributor of industrial hoses. After I met with and spoke to various customers and employees, the company recognized that by having sales quote installations of hoses in isolation of service, they were not only losing money but more importantly, detracting from the customer's experience. Every time a service technician delivered or installed a hose, they would become frustrated and vocal when the hose itself wouldn't fit, often having to leave the customer's site mid-installation. This would result in delays in installation and, in some instances, even additional cost (if they chose not to absorb the cost themselves). Being brave, the president of the industrial hose division went against the industry norms, the feedback of his peers, and pushback by many of his longstanding employees in order to ensure that sales and service worked together on quoting customer installations, resulting in higher upfront costs. He reshaped his culture by breaking down barriers between two working groups that had a long history and rivalry by placing sales and service together. The results, however, coming from pairing up both sales and service for the purposes of quoting new customer projects, were not only reduced downtime and additional costs, but also an improved customer experience. Indirectly, the changes made also led to an increase in customer retention and growth in customer referrals, which further influenced opportunities for more sales and new business.

If the examples of how a retail business such as Hillberg and Berk or an industrial supply company can be brave and reshape their culture in order to grow their sales and revenue don't convince you, let's look at another situation. In Chapter 11, we were introduced to Michael Beneteau and his team at CenterLine. As a manufacturer of automation, CenterLine sells to industrial customers. Regardless, Michael and his team realize that it's all about providing a positive customer experience, so much so that "customer first," their empowered brand, has been built to ensure that a customer's experience with them is far superior to any other they might have. This is why Michael and his team work diligently to ensure that the culture of their employees is not only to understand the philosophy of "customer first," but that they naturally place their customer first in everything they do, from design, to manufacturing, to installation and training. Michael and his team, like other unstoppable organizations, recognize that they must be brave in shaping a culture that not only satisfies customers today, but is prepared to satisfy customers and employees of tomorrow.

How Culture Grows Market Share

With our discussions around culture, then, you are likely wondering how taking the steps outlined here in reshaping your own culture can directly result in increasing market share. Well, it won't if you simply stop with a focus on creating an exceptional customer experience. Although good for existing customers, this approach won't help you attract any new customers and capture market share from your competitors.

Creating a culture that lives the "customer first" brand and ensures an "exceptional customer experience" for every interaction means that your employees truly believe, embrace, and promote everything wonderful that your organization is doing, and there is no better resource for promoting the value your customers are experiencing than your employees. I'm not suggesting blatantly promoting your efforts per say, but "If you don't toot your own horn, don't complain that there is no music," to quote Guy Kawasaki.[3] This is where all of the benefits of your efforts thus far in becoming an unstoppable organization begin to pay off. Because as we've outlined in previous chapters, if you've created an environment in which your employees are empowered, then they will be highly engaged, and in being so they are in the best position to promote all of the benefits of your organization. Taking from the various interviews and interactions I've had with unstoppable organizations, here is a list of just a few ways in which their employees are helping to promote the brand, products, services, and value of their organizations:

- Sharing company information and promotions on social media.
- Donning company apparel (that employees have paid for themselves!) at events outside of work.
- Gifting customers with various products (like the sparkle ball) that their employers offer.
- Speaking on behalf of their employer at events and functions.

- Posting positive reviews of their employer on sites such as Glassdoor.com.
- Purchasing their company's products or services for their own family and friends.
- Participating in community activities that indirectly promote their company's benefits.
- Recommending to friends and family to apply and join their employer.
- Supporting and sponsoring community and regional causes and events.
- Defending their employer in the media when negativity arises.
- Bringing ideas forward to their employers on how to further increase their brand awareness.

Similarly, by creating exceptional customer experiences through your employees, you reap the benefits of growing market share as a direct result of your customer's efforts. Examples that several of the unstoppable organizations have shared with me in how their customers are helping them to grow their market share include:

- Sharing products, promotions, and company news on social media.
- Posting positively glowing reviews of your products on your organization's Websites, as well as that of other resellers or partners.
- Posting negative reviews on your competition's Website, identifying your organization's product or service as being superior.
- Joining and participating in a community of your followers, sharing their experiences and ideas on your organization's blog, social media pages, or other forums.
- Purchasing and wearing apparel that displays your brand and organizational information.
- Publishing articles and posts relating to a positive experience with your organization.
- Attending events held by your organization and inviting other friends, family, and coworkers to join.

- Introducing friends and family members to your products or services.

For more ideas, tips, and bonus materials to help you grow your market share through your employees, make sure to visit *www.unstoppable organization.com.*

There are literally dozens more I could mention, but what's important to realize is this: when you are brave in building a culture that places your customer first, ensuring each has an exceptional experience, not only do you create customers who are raving fans of your organization and its products (which is essentially free marketing), but you also create such a buzz both internally with employees and externally with customers that would-be customers can't help but notice. The resulting impact is capturing market share. Referring back to an earlier example, I can't help but think about Harley Davidson. How can an organization sell their product for two to three times more than their competitor and continue to grow their market share after more than 100 years in business? It takes a good product, yes (Harley was once known for a poor product), and good marketing, yes (Harley has only in recent years become a good marketer). But what is outstanding about Harley Davidson is the sheer amount of positive information that their customers and employees share. Visit any dealership and you'll be overwhelmed at how friendly and nonaggressive everyone is. Riders create their own clubs, their own rides, and tout the benefits by purchasing and wearing Harley Davidson apparel. It really is a marvel to experience. Owning my own Harley, I have become somewhat addicted to the brand myself. This is empowering your market share, and it is another key distinction between the average organization and an unstoppable one.

Lessons from Unstoppable Organizations

In order to dominate over their competition, unstoppable organizations help to spread the word of their products and services, and in turn appeal to a continuing growing number of customers by enticing employees and existing customers to support spread the word about the value they offer.

PART 4 GROWING FORWARD

In Part 3, we discussed the importance of "thinking forward." With this concept in mind, this book would be useless if it didn't consider addressing some emerging and growing trends that includes uncovering exactly what unstoppable organizations are doing to prepare for and ensure they dominate in the coming years. Recognizing how empowerment is being used by the organizations such as Blommer Chocolate, Hillberg and Berk, Saje Natural Wellness, and CenterLine to guarantee customers have an exceptional experience, increasing market awareness, competitive distinction, and value for both employees and customers makes sense. Consider the speed of evolution and the continued influence of technology on all sectors and industries. Exactly what are these organizations doing to prepare for the long-term? In Part 4, we discuss the evolution of how companies market and sell their products and services; identifying key distinctions in areas that will be critical to success in the coming decade. We explore the approaches that some of today's most successful organizations are applying in order to capture an increased market share in the coming decade. For those wanting to gain an advantage over the competition, this part is for you.

13

EMPLOYEES: REAL GROWTH HORMONE FOR YOUR BUSINESS

Happy employees lead to happy customers,
which leads to more profits.
Vaughn Aust, EVP of Integrated Solutions, MarketStar

If there's anything you've come to realize by this point, it's that unstoppable organizations which are growing their customers, revenue, and success on a continuum have fully adopted and deployed various approaches that, in turn, empower their organization and the people within it. They've empowered their customers by enticing them to become involved in identifying their own preferred experience, ensuring that customer feedback on ideas and improvements are not only solicited, but also integrated into the development and delivery of products and services. They've empowered their employees by connecting them and their organizations with a common purpose, and building a culture that provides them with more authority and autonomy to make decisions to satisfy customers. They've empowered their brand by creating and connecting their employee-facing brand with their customer-facing brand, focusing first on attracting and appealing to employees in order to make the organization attractive and appealing to customers. They've also empowered their market share, getting employees and customers involved in helping spread the word not only about the great products or services, but also what a great place it is to work and a great community to be a part of.

From the examples of organizations we've shared, you've likely noted that each is at varying levels of organizational maturity, some having been in the market place for more than 100 years, whereas others have been around less than 10 years. Regardless, organizations we've dissected, both new and old, have achieved significant growth despite economic and market forces by empowering various aspects of their organization. My intention in sharing with you such a wide variety of examples is to dispel any misconceptions or myths you may have relative to empowerment being a strategy that is only possible in organizations that are at a specific level of maturity. Although this possibly isn't a concern of yours (and it shouldn't be), all too often I have been told that either empowerment is only possible in young organizations who are just starting out, or on the contrary, it is only possible in organizations that are mature and stable. Both statements, extremes by nature, are false as we have proven throughout this book.

This said, in order to successfully introduce the various empowerment strategies we've discussed, some consideration should be made relative to the level of maturity of an organization and specific to where to begin, how quickly to move, and what targets are realistic. To be clear, however, there is no "ideal" level of maturity an organization must have to succeed. This means that now is always the best time to introduce empowerment in order to drive higher revenues, capture more market share, and gain new customers. It's for this reason that in this chapter we will discuss three starting points to introduce empowerment specifically focused on small businesses: mid-market privately held organizations, large privately held organizations, and publicly traded organizations. We will discuss how each of these organizations should position themselves to adopt the ideas and approaches set forth in this book in order to empower employees and address building a more robust brand awareness, creating stronger employee-customer connections, and constructing a stronger collaboration amongst customer-facing roles. This is no small feat, but nonetheless it's very achievable and, as I'm sure you've assessed from our discussions thus far, absolutely necessary if you want your organization to survive and thrive in the coming decades. Before we dive into how each of these organizations should begin their quest to success, let's first ensure a few things are clear, as they are necessary for success along your empowerment journey.

Stop Looking for Growth in Isolation

I began this book discussing many of the misnomers relative to growing an organization that most leaders today get sucked into believing are the reasons for their lack of sustained growth. You've likely heard and experienced this yourself, with experts shouting from the rooftops about a focus on improving sales closing rates, becoming better at referrals, or improving marketing presence as being the solutions that will lead to growth. These so-called experts and their opinions aren't wrong necessarily, but their view of growth in isolation is both risky and, more often than not, unsustainable. Consider, for example, that more inbound referrals on a regular basis will increase sales opportunities, but are a fast road to nowhere if the inbound leads aren't convinced to buy, committed to buy, and content with the product or service itself. Along the same lines, increasing your sales team's ability to track or close leads is a complete waste of energy if the experience the customer has once they've been closed and become a customer is less than stellar. These are simply examples of looking for growth in isolation, failing to consider the sheer importance of ensuring that every customer's experience is exceptional.

Possibly your organization is struggling with similar ideas, that the inability to achieve sales and revenue growth targets are a direct correlation to a specific function, role, or area within the business. If this is the case, I would first recommend sharing a copy of this book with them. Don't try to convince them that growth in isolation is a path to nowhere, but rather help them see and hear how unstoppable organizations are growing leaps and bounds by focusing on the various strategies and tactics we've discussed. Next, I would recommend interviewing the customers directly.

To confirm that your organization isn't pursuing activities to grow in isolation, let's complete a simple exercise to confirm such. Feel free to engage in any of these activities individually or collectively to assess your organization's current state:

1. Visit with the leaders of your sales team, your marketing team, and your customer service team, and ask them what training is planned for employees this year, and in what areas of discipline. If training is being delivered with a specific department or segment in the organization, then this is an example of growth in isolation.

2. Check in with executives across the organization and ask with whom they plan to engage this year, as a consultant, contractor, or advisor, and what the objectives of the engagement look like. Once again, engaging someone in this way to focus on typically a single area of the business is an example of seeking growth or improvement in isolation.

3. Poke your head into different departments and determine to what extent each department is investing time in cross-training, helping individuals from other departments understand how their team functions and its specific goals and objectives.

4. Drop by some team meetings and see who is there that belongs on another team. Are sales people sitting in your customer service team meetings? Are marketing people spending time in the sales meetings? The degree of interface of various departments in a meeting is a means to measure the extent of isolation that is occurring in your organization.

Whether you decide to complete this activity or simply reflect upon it, I'm sure you'll conclude that, at least to some degree, there are activities occurring within your organization right now that attempt growth in isolation. Some of the more common examples of what you might find include:

-   Meetings and communications shared only amongst a select group or employees.
-   Training applied to only a cross-section of employees.
-   Misaligned departmental goals and objectives.
-   Lack of cross-training amongst departments.

- Limited access by internal working groups to connect with customers.
- Limited access by external facing working groups to understand business operations.

Unfortunately, it's these activities and the silos they create that result in various working groups, departments, and leaders chasing new solutions, opportunities, and ideas that, in turn, spark the very activities and focus toward growth in isolation. The key to achieving growth and becoming unstoppable, as we've identified throughout this book, is to do so through *collaboration*.

Collaborative Selling: The Best Sales Strategy Involves Those Outside Sales

The other consideration that you must not only understand but agree upon, aligned with the concept that doing anything in isolation within an organization is detrimental to growth, is that collaboration is absolutely crucial to success. From our earlier discussions, particularly in Part 3, we discussed how growth results from collaboration both within the organization and, externally, in engaging with key stakeholders. When it comes to sales and selling, then, taking a collaborative approach means that individuals who work in or support sales or selling are not the only ones responsible for sales. In addition, to ensure sales of products or services, the individuals in these departments never work, train, or meet in isolation of other departments or groups to identify strategies and tactics to achieve sales targets, but rather collaborate with various departments, individuals, and stakeholders from across the organization in order to support growth.

Last year, I was asked to speak to a leadership team of a distributor of household products. The organization sold their manufacturers' products directly to retailers on behalf of manufacturers. When I met with the CEO and vice president of sales, they identified the need to grow their sales revenue, and in turn wanted me to "pump up" the sales team. "Not a problem," I responded, "who will be joining us in this session?"

The response was, "Our sales department, of course." Wrong answer. Sales and selling are not isolated events. Remember my earlier example of the industrial hose distributor who was trying to sell hoses, but doing so at a loss? Their view was that service (who installed the hoses) was a separate group from sales (who sold the hoses), and the result of this view and approach was a loss of profits from sales being made on account of misquoting, rework, and delays. I advised the CEO and his vice president that the only way we were going to achieve their objectives of gaining commitment from their team for pursuing and achieving higher sales and revenue growth was to bring in not only the sales department, but representatives from all departments that supported sales. In their situation, this included employees from marketing, customer service, distribution, and business development. With this broader team together, we went about getting the group engaged in sharing ideas and strategies that would result in not only more sales, but higher revenue and increased profitability. This is the key to collaborative selling. A company can always sell more by focusing in isolation on better sales techniques or stronger marketing campaigns, but the resulting revenue is often lower than the desired targets, mainly because the strategies identified and deployed are disconnected from the key areas that deliver on sales commitments.

The CEOs of the various unstoppable organizations whom I've discussed throughout this book have all built a foundation around collaborative selling, which is the idea that every employee has a role to play to make sure customers know about the brand and buy the products. In turn, this ensures that the customers' experience is exceptional so they return again and again. They recognize that making sales to a customer is a team sport and best achieved through organizational collaboration.

The concepts behind collaborative selling that these CEOs employ include the following:

- Employees that are hired into the organization are first and foremost a cultural fit for the organization, its customers, and specifically the team they will be working with. Skills needed to do a job are something that can be learned, but cultural fit is crucial to success, no excuses.
- Every employee must understand how their roles directly and indirectly influence a customer's experience of the organization's products or services. In this way, every employee guarantees that their customer has a great experience.

- Employees are educated continuously on what customers value, how this value is shifting, and how living the organizational values and purpose support consistently delivering it.
- Ongoing cross-training of employees in various roles and departments outside of their own to learn and stay abreast of how other employees impact the customer's experience, and how both roles working more effectively together supports the collaborative approach and reduces the tendency for gaps in perceptions.
- Employee meetings and various other communications with and amongst employees are held cross-functionally, blending meetings and discussions amongst various departments and teams to ensure a continuous understanding of the challenges, issues, and value each department brings.

What's important to point out as well is that applying and practicing these concepts in building a collaborative approach to selling costs virtually nothing. That's right, there is no cost to collaboration, yet the outcomes and value both the organization and its customers receive are priceless.

Here's another example on how important a collaborative approach is and how little it can cost. A few years ago, I was asked by a mid-sized manufacturer to look at their sales processes and approach to identify what improvements might be necessary. After initially speaking with several customers, sales reps, and employees in sales, customer service, marketing, production, and distribution the issue became clear. Everyone, from the internal sales team, the external sales reps, and customer service were working their butts off to improve sales, but they were doing so in isolation. This was creating competing priorities, wasting time, and ultimately having a negative impact on the customer's experience.

Sales was working hard to grow and close deals, but in doing so they were isolating the sales reps who were often calling on the same customers. This created a mixed message and led to a lack of trust on behalf of customers, as they felt like everyone was trying to sell them something.

Customer service was working diligently to deal with customer issues and concerns while processing orders, but found that sales was often making promises the organization couldn't deliver, meaning they were in the role of advising both the customer and the internal sales rep that what the customer wanted simply wasn't possible. The customer felt lied to, and in some instances, chose never to connect with their sales agent again.

Sales reps were effectively doing their best to find and track down new leads, but were isolated from staff in the office, often misrepresenting what the company could reasonably achieve in the way of lead-times, product quality, and customization. The internal sales team thought the reps were doing this just to make a sale, but in reality they were misinformed. The customer, of course, suffered once again as a result.

The more you instill and support collaboration amongst employees and other stakeholders around the sales and revenue growth objectives of your organization, the better chance you'll have of achieving them. This is not a new idea, I realize, but one that I find is rarely adopted. In my view, it's essentially selling for dummies. You don't need to be a sales guru to understand that by helping everyone in the organization understand the role they have in influencing the customer's experience and then support them in creating an environment in which they can work together, the better chance you'll have of not only higher sales, but higher profitability with each sale.

Building Your Secret Sales Force

Interestingly, the concept of collaborative selling is so straightforward, yet so underpracticed and underappreciated by so many organizations that I've encountered, that I like to tell those who actually adopt the approaches we've discussed they are building a "secret sales force." I coined this term for a few reasons:

1. All employees have the opportunity to make or break a customer relationship based on what they do and how they do it.
2. The most successful sales are those that meet the customer's needs in a way that ensures not only does the customer want to engage with the organization's products or service again, but is willing and enthused about telling others how great your organization is.
3. There is no sense in selling anything if you can't do so profitably. When employees are clear on how their roles influence

not only the customer's experience, but also the ability of an organization to sell and deliver a product or service cost effectively, they are empowered to ensure every transaction is profitable. To do otherwise, regardless of reasoning, is simply a willingness to step into the short line toward going broke.

In summary, when every employee in an organization is clear on what customers need and want, they understand how their role can add to and support a positive customer experience; they have the ability to make decisions without hesitation about supporting the customer and doing their job as effectively as possible; and they are constantly involved in and enticed to collaborate with others both inside and outside the organization to make the customer's experience progressively better. Thus, the only possible outcome is a group of employees committed to sales and selling.

For additional resources and bonus materials to help you build your secret sales force, make sure you visit *www.unstoppableorganization.com*.

There is more to becoming an unstoppable organization than building a secret sales force, and with these foundational concepts now fully explained, let's identify specifically how your organization, regardless of its size or maturity, can fully adopt and integrate empowerment and collaborative selling in order to join the list of unstoppable organizations.

Unstoppable Growth: Empowering Your Organization to Grow

As I mentioned at the start of this chapter, the idea that what a smaller or mid-market organization needs to do to take a more collaborative approach to growth and in turn build their secret sales force is often very different than what a large publicly traded company needs to do. For the purposes of our discussions, I've outlined the action steps for each of these organizations in the following and created definitions for each differently sized organization. Feel free to make your own assessment as to which category you fit in based on the brief description below each. It's less important to consider where to start than it is to actually start. In addition, recognizing that some of these steps may already be employed within your organization to varying degrees, I've outlined the top five priorities that should be focused on and fully adopted, rather than specific steps to take.

Small Business: 3 to 50 Employees

These are businesses where the owner(s) are working and building up their teams while growing their business. Often, there is very little capital available to support employee training, as it needs to be reinvested in the business itself. On the positive side, small businesses have the ability to make decisions and shifts quickly on account of their nimbleness and youth in their space.

Priority 1: Ensure all employees fit well within the team environment. Be willing to train the right person in developing the necessary skills.

Priority 2: Ensure cross-training is adopted so you have a few employees as specialists and the majority as generalists. Not only does this create variety for employees, it also protects the owners in the event an employee leaves or becomes ill.

Priority 3: Share openly with employees on a quarterly basis the opportunities and objectives for growth, and help them understand how they can contribute. Make the discussion less focused on revenue and more heavily focused around growth of the business, providing sustained employment for the employees and an opportunity to continue to learn and shift into new roles.

Priority 4: Avoid hiring "managers" to oversee employees, but rather identify team-leads, those people who have the greatest experience amongst employees and who invariably get along with and are respected by others.

Priority 5: Introduce daily meetings or "huddles" with employees to discuss the priorities for the day and to allow employees a chance to raise questions and concerns. Seek to build collaboration amongst the team in resolving issues; don't jump in and try to fix everything yourself.

Mid-Sized Organizations: 50 to 1000 Employees

These are organizations that often have one or two facilities and contain multiple departments centered on operations, sales, customer service, and finance to name a few. The organization has both managers and some frontline leaders (either supervisors or team leaders) in place to lead teams, and has some infrastructure in the way of documented procedures and processes for employees to follow. In addition, it's likely that software platforms such as ERP and CRM (customer relationship management) exist.

Priority 1: As employees grow in number, leaders are increasingly important in order to ensure that employees and departments are working collaboratively. It's at this point that there is a risk that leaders begin to "manage" employees versus support their development and growth. As a result, leaders, be they managers, supervisors, or otherwise, need to fully understand their own personal behaviors and communication, and understand how these have influence (good or bad) on others. This can be achieved through completion and understanding of tools such as incorporating a DiSC or Myers-Briggs assessment. The key is to increase awareness.

Priority 2: As mid-sized organizations grow, more layers of management are often introduced. As a result, senior executives become disconnected from how the business actually runs. To counteract this, ensure frequent interactions between executive leaders within the organization and frontline employees. Increase awareness of how employee roles influence customers directly and indirectly while also making sure executive leaders understand the challenges and frustrations experienced by employees on the frontlines.

Priority 3: Growth to this level also often results in communications becoming more isolated. As a result, it's necessary to increase communications across the organization by creating more frequent collaborative meetings amongst all departments. Openly share priorities and issues, and determine how collective actions across departments can resolve issues and improve the customer's experience.

Priority 4: Create connections between departments by frequently rotating employees from one department into another. For example, have someone from accounting spend 30 days working with the sales department, understanding the various roles and ensuring they are exposed to customers in various ways. Spread out the 30-day increments through a period of several months and make sure that all employees have this experience.

Priority 5: As organizations grow, they often become increasingly disconnected with customers. For this reason, regularly solicit customer feedback on various products, services, and ideas to identify what changes or improvements are necessary as the organization grows.

Large Sized Organizations: Greater Than 1000 Employees

These are organizations with multiple locations, often spread out globally. Their breadth and depth of customers are highly diverse, as are their employees. They have highly complex software and technology in place to support sharing of information.

Priority 1: Customer needs are so broad and diverse it's often difficult for employees to connect with what customers need or want. It's critical to help employees understand the general influence their roles play in supporting current customers and bringing on new ones. Leaders must continuously focus on helping to make this connection.

Priority 2: Leaders are often focused heavily on corporate objectives versus employee developmental objectives. To make sure employees remain engaged, leaders at all levels need to remain aware of their influence on employees (using tools such as DiSC or Myers-Briggs) and, in turn, use this awareness to stay connected with them.

Priority 3: When an organization grows to this size, engagement becomes difficult to manage on account of so many employees working with so many different leaders. It's crucial that senior leaders invest time working in various departments, connecting with employees, asking about how the environment could be improved, and taking rapid action to support such.

Priority 4: Further to the previous priority, in order for employees to remain engaged, it's crucial that leaders focus on employee empowerment, building employee confidence with the ability to make decisions in isolation, and ensuring the continued effectiveness in their roles.

Priority 5: Attracting and retaining employees at this size can be as much of a challenge as attracting and retaining customers, guaranteeing that time and effort is invested in capturing employees' commitment to the organization and allowing them to support building the brand.

As I've outlined several times in this book, if you're finding it difficult to assess which category your organization fits into, or which priorities to begin with, don't worry about it. What's important is that you start introducing the concepts of empowerment now, making adjustments and improvements as you go, rather than get caught up in what to do or when to start. This is a journey, so there will be plenty of ups and downs; however, starting now will mean you are already ahead of your competition who is still considering what they should do next.

Lessons from Unstoppable Organizations

Unstoppable organizations understand that the more they can help their employees to collaborate and interact with each other, avoiding isolated activities and silos and, in turn, helping them to learn from each other, the greater opportunity the organization will have to satisfy customers while growing their employees' knowledge and experience.

14

SOCIAL MEDIA: STRATEGY VERSUS DISTRACTION

Distracted from distraction by distraction.
Thomas Stearns Elliot, Literary and Social Critic

I would be remiss if I wrote this book about how unstoppable organizations are growing with and through their people and didn't make a brief mention of social media, a powerful tool that many of the organizations I interviewed and interacted with during the past several years are using in various ways. What I've learned is that, as social media platforms come and go, it has become increasingly difficult for most CEOs, executives, and leaders to assess which platforms work best, and more importantly, where and how they should deploy a platform in order to reap a quantifiable benefit of some sort. In this chapter, I discuss how to determine which platforms unstoppable organizations are deploying, how they are using them to support their growth, and what risks or pitfalls they have experienced.

How Unstoppable Organizations Use Social Media

To begin with, there are generally three ways in which the unstoppable organizations I work with are using social media: as a marketing tool to attract and connect with customers; a tool to engage with and increase communication amongst their employees; and as a method to connect with and appeal to potential employees. The most common use is in marketing. In a time when more and more customers are researching, comparing, and buying online, social media offers an often cost-effective means of engaging with customers. The powerhouse tools that most unstoppable organizations use, in no particular order, include the following:

1. LinkedIn: Having a company page that their customers can visit to learn more about the organization, its affiliations, and initiatives, as well as its products or services. As a free version, the information that is contained on a company page is generic, but some organizations are using the paid versions of LinkedIn to build up a better profile with images, links, video, and written content that is more appealing and interactive.

2. Twitter: Providing frequent tweets on company updates, customer successes, and product or service initiatives means Twitter provides a free method of sending out information in a brief format, which can include images and hyperlinks back to the organization's Website or other relevant online platforms.

3. Facebook: Typically the more controversial platform, it is seen by some organizations as more retail-oriented versus supporting relationships in a business-to-business market. Yet having a company page on Facebook is free, and it offers a way to share content and images that are more personalized, allowing organizations to connect with their customers on a one-to-one basis.

4. Instagram: Typically used as a tool to share images only, it allows organizations to share exciting news on their products, services, customers, and even office shenanigans in a way that can be enticing to customers as it builds a stronger connection with the culture and offerings of an organization.

5. YouTube: Continually becoming more popular as organizations incorporate it to share product or service features and functions, YouTube is often seen as a great tool for creating "how-to" videos and sharing them with customers at virtually no cost other than video production or editing.

As you can imagine, the common theme amongst the unstoppable organizations throughout this book is that they are active on social media. Less common are which platforms organizations prefer to use, and specifically, how they are incorporating these and others which I haven't included, such as Snapchat or Pinterest.

Being active, of course, means different things to different organizations and different people, but when I asked many of the CEOs why they were active on social media, their responses were almost identical:

- Social media is a way to get in front of our customers and employees at virtually no cost.
- Social media is a key strategy when considering how to build a brand and community in today's online marketplace.
- As future generations grow up with the Internet as their preferred communication means, being present and active on social media is critical to long-term growth and success.

Creating Stronger Customer-Employee Connections Through Social Media

What is also common amongst the unstoppable organizations that I interact with is their preference to be active on social media, rather than just have a presence. If they were using Twitter, for example, they didn't just schedule tweets to go out each day or week, but always ensured that someone monitored Twitter to respond to anyone who made an inquiry. Presence, when it comes to social media, is what ensures the "social" aspect is something that can be capitalized on. Not being active and social online is the fastest way to ruin a customer relationship. Consider that there are more and more customers online today and that, to them, sending a tweet with a request or "shout-out" to their favorite brand that goes unanswered or ignored, is no different than failing to respond to an e-mail or not answering the phone. The CEOs, executives, and leaders of unstoppable organizations recognize that being active on social media is increasingly a given as younger generations adapt and shift their communication preferences. Where someone older is just as likely to send an e-mail or call if their Facebook message goes unanswered, someone of a younger generation is more likely to simply stop pursuing or interacting with an organization.

On the positive side, being active on social media, organizations can create stronger connections with their customers, who share their excitement and pride. This is where the power of social media comes into play, becoming a marketing force to be reckoned with. Where an organization might have once invested from thousands to tens of thousands of dollars on marketing in radio or television ads, which are one-directional, they can now invest mere hundreds of dollars to sponsor ads on Facebook or Snapchat, reaching just as broad an audience. Moreover, they have the chance to engage directly in dialogue with customers by posing questions and responding to inquiries.

Social media marketing is, in fact, one of the best interactive media tools for marketing to and interacting with customers that exist today, helping organizations to create the stronger customer-employee connections that I referenced in earlier chapters.

Engaging Employees on Social Media

In addition to the benefits social media can have in supporting engagement and dialogue with customers, it also offers the very same benefits to engage with employees. To help foster a culture built around purpose and employees, Rachel Mielke's team uses a simple (and free) Facebook group to engage and entice employees to work, collaborate, and celebrate together. The Facebook group offers a way for employees to engage in a dynamic environment rather than a static one, meaning information that is shared is live, current, and can contain multiple media forms to improve communication between team members. Although Mielke says they are now looking closely at Facebook's new "workplace" platform[1] to further the benefits that Facebook offers, she and her team stand behind using social media to engage existing employees in ways that were never possible before by allowing them to open up and share a more personal connection not only with coworkers, but also with leaders across the organization, including Mielke herself.

In addition to incorporating social media as a tool to replace historically popular communication methods such as e-mail, the benefits that social media provides in creating a stronger team also extend externally. Consider, for example, that LinkedIn's Global Talent Trends reported as recently as 2015 the following statistics as they relate to the potential employee's use of social media in finding a new job:

- "Social professional networks are the number one source of quality hires."
- "Over 75% of people who recently changed jobs used LinkedIn to inform their career decision."
- "New employees sourced through LinkedIn are 40% less likely to leave the company within the first six months."[2]

In addition to the direct benefits that a platform like LinkedIn can offer to attract and identify new hires, involving employees in your social media strategy can assist in building an online presence that not only appeals to potential customers, but also potential employees. A close friend of mine is quite active on Facebook, posting personal stories and pictures several times each day. At least once each week she shares a post her employer has published on their Facebook page, invariably touting the achievements the organization has had, the success of its employees, and the organization's involvement in the community. She also shares "we're hiring" posts to her entire network of at least 200 friends. Consider the power this has, because the 200 friends who see these posts can also share with their friends, who can share with their friends, and so on. Engaging on social media both directly and indirectly with your employees is a great way to build public recognition of the benefits and positive attributes of your organization, as well as solicit support and assistance from the public. This, in turn, can lead to attracting new talent—and all at a cost of $0, with the exception of having someone actually publish the posts.

If you want to become an unstoppable organization, then social media is a tool that you need to introduce, be active on, and use to interact with both your customers and employees. Not doing so, particularly as we continue to be connected more and more online, can be detrimental to your growth and even your survival.

For additional tips and bonus resources, make sure to visit *www .unstoppableorganization.com.*

Lessons from Unstoppable Organizations

The leaders of unstoppable organizations recognize that social media is first and foremost social, and as a result, they make sure that the platforms they use are those that their customers are engaged in, but also that the same platforms are managed in a way that allow customers to interact with employees to further support an exceptional customer experience.

15

GROWTH 6.0: PEER INTO MY CRYSTAL BALL

Growth is never by mere chance; it is the
result of forces working together.

James Cash Penney

At this point you're likely wondering, so where do we "grow" from here? Throughout this book, I've mentioned that unstoppable organizations are always thinking forward. Considering the ground we've covered, I believe it's important to share some predictions with you regarding the future to assist you in doing the same.

For this final chapter, let's revisit a few of the key points already discussed, making some predictions about further shifts or changes that are likely to influence your organization in the coming years.

The Top 10 Predictions for Unstoppable Organizations

Here are my top 10 predictions that will influence the marketplace, its customers, and employees in the coming decade, in no particular order:

1. The value customers place in one-to-one personalized interactions will continue to grow, allowing organizations that provide exceptional and personalized experiences the ability to capture significant market share over their competitors.

2. Employees will aggressively seek out new employment with organizations that allow them the chance to grow personally and professionally in an environment that is fun, challenging, and rewarding.

3. E-mail as the predominant communication tool amongst organizations will disappear as new social tools such as Facebook Workplace provide a more dynamic means of communication through multiple media in real-time.

4. The hierarchy of management, made popular in the Industrial Age, will disappear, replaced by cross-functional teams that are empowered to collaborate in an environment in which they self-manage.

5. The CEOs and executives who are successful will be those who collaborate and work side-by-side with their employees, building a future together rather than in isolation.

6. Technology that is the most in demand for organizations will be that which is most effective at building repositories of information based on employee discussions and dialogue, replacing written procedures and policies with knowledge repositories.

7. What organizations stand for will become the defining point at which they appeal to customers and employees alike. "Walking the talk" will determine the longevity and success an organization achieves.

8. The number of family-owned businesses will increase as the "monetary returns first" reputation of private equity firms falls out of favor with customers and employees, who prefer a more "family friendly" atmosphere.

9. Organizations that support their employees in becoming versed in multiple roles and skill sets, providing diversity in both experience and knowledge, will become the employers of choice and will, in turn, provide more value for their customers.

10. Compensation will continue to be a less important variable when it comes to attracting and retaining employees. Instead, those organizations that provide ample free time to employees for personal priorities will be a more appealing choice as newer generations seek a more balanced and fulfilling life.

Final Thoughts

Throughout this book I've shared various exercises that you can complete at any time regardless of the size, maturity level, market, or sector your organization is within. There are a few points I want to emphasize as you begin this journey on your own. Consider these guidelines to empowering your organization:

1. There is nothing more important to your future growth than your employees. The culture you build, the environment you create, and the extent to which you allow employees to manage their work in support of achieving and delivering on customer value is of the most importance.

2. Customer needs and desires are changing; by interacting more frequently with customers and soliciting their feedback (and then acting promptly on that feedback), you can stay ahead of your competition.

3. Attracting and retaining the best employees for your organization and its customers relies on creating an environment in which they prefer to work. This will mean throwing accepted norms out of the window and, instead, challenging your organization to shift toward satisfying employee preferences.

4. The growth of any organization is not based on being good at selling or marketing, but rather being good at building a collaborative team that rapidly responds to customer needs and desires. The more you can help employees embrace how their

role adds value to customers, and so empower employees with autonomy in supporting customers, the faster your organization will grow.

5. It is less important how you begin your empowerment journey and more so that you just begin. Start anywhere, but start now. Simple steps are the best way to begin your journey, and will allow you the freedom and ability to make adjustments as you progress.

For a downloadable version of your own empowerment plan, make sure to visit *www.unstoppableorganization.com*.

I wrote this book for a simple reason. Too many organizations today are failing to grow because they are focused on doing the wrong things. This is not to say they aren't trying or that the people that lead or work for most organizations don't have the best of intentions. What it takes to grow an organization in today's market place is very different than what it was only 10 or 20 years ago. Don't fall prey to bad advice.

It is my hope that by sharing more than a dozen stories and examples of what organizations are doing to grow, you will be able to take the fastest route possible to growth and, in turn, build an unstoppable organization.

NOTES

Chapter 1

1. David Blaine is a well-known magician, endurance artist, and illusionist.
2. "20 years inside the mind of the CEO . . . What's next?" PwC.com, www.pwc.com/gx/en/ceo-survey/2017/pwc-ceo-20th-survey -report-2017.pdf.

Chapter 2

1. Sir Winston Leonard Spencer-Churchill was a British politician who served as the Prime Minister of the United Kingdom from 1940 to 1945 and again from 1951 to 1955.
2. Maslow's (1943, 1954) hierarchy of needs is a motivational theory in psychology comprising a five-tier model of human needs.

Chapter 3

1. Spencer Soper, "More Than 50% of Shoppers Turn First to Amazon in Product Search," September 27, 2016, www.bloomberg.com/news/articles/2016-09-27/ more-than-50-of-shoppers-turn-first-to-amazon-in-product-search.
2. See: www.stripe.com.

Chapter 4

1. Howard Shultz is the founder and chairman of Starbucks Coffee.
2. *The Founder*, directed by John Lee Hancock. Released: August 18, 2016.
3. Richard and Maurice McDonald are the founders of the first McDonald's restaurant.
4. "United Breaks Guitars," https://en.wikipedia.org/wiki/United_Breaks_Guitars.

Chapter 5

1. See: www.flightstats.com.
2. Claude Shannon, Brainyquote.com, www.brainyquote.com/authors/claude_shannon.
3. Laura Entis, "10 Top CEOs on What's Changing About the World of Work," March 27, 2017, http://fortune.com/2017/03/27/best-companies-ceos-workforce/.

Chapter 6

1. Amy Drew, "Talkin' About Your Generation," www.psychologicalscience.org/observer/talkin-about-your-generation#.WUaISsmQwdU.
2. "Baby boomers," https://en.wikipedia.org/wiki/Baby_boomers.
3. Patrick J. Kiger, "10 Events That Influenced Generation X," February 13, 2016, http://tvblogs.nationalgeographic.com/2016/02/13/10-events-that-influenced-generation-x/.
4. Andrea Caumont, "What would you name today's youngest generation of American?" March 12, 2014, www.pewresearch.org/fact-tank/2014/03/12/what-would-you-name-todays-youngest-generation-of-americans/.
5. Shannon Greenwood, Andrew Perrin, and Maeve Duggan, "Social Media Update 2016," November 11, 2016, www.pewinternet.org/2016/11/11/social-media-update-2016/.
6. See: https://ca.blackberry.com/.
7. See: www.humber.ca/about-humber/.
8. Robin Lewis, "Millennials: Double Trouble for Retail," April 30, 2014, www.forbes.com/sites/robinlewis/2014/04/30/millennials-double-trouble-for-retail/#712302bb1d8e.

9. See: www.immersionactive.com/item/stats-facts/.
10. "Gen Xers the Biggest Online Retail Spenders, Gen Y Most Connected," December 21, 2012, www.marketingcharts.com/uncategorized/gen-xers-the-biggest-online-retail-spenders-gen-y-most-connected-25594/.
11. "Deloitte Study: Digital Influences More than $1 Trillion in Retail Store Sales," April 28, 2014, www.prnewswire.com/news-releases/deloitte-study-digital-influences-more-than-1-trillion-in-retail-store-sales-256967501.html.
12. Ibid.
13. Jiafeng Li, Study: Online Shopping Behavior in the Digital Era," May 10, 2013, www.iacquire.com/blog/study-online-shopping-behavior-in-the-digital-era.
14. "Story of the Week: Zappos' Tony Hsieh," November 2013, http://projects.wsj.com/soty/week/21/story-of-the-week--zappos-tony-hsieh.

Chapter 7

1. Amy Adkins, "Millennials: The Job-Hopping Generation," May 12, 2016, www.gallup.com/businessjournal/191459/millennials-job-hopping-generation.aspx.

Chapter 8

1. Dave Carroll, "United Breaks Guitars," www.youtube.com/watch?v=5YGc4zOqozo.

Chapter 9

1. See: www.amazon.com/gp/help/customer/display.html?nodeId=200444160.
2. See: www.wedishowersystems.com/.
3. See: www.mudstyle.com/?c=about.
4. Jim Edwards, "Check Out The Insane Lengths Zappos Customer Service Reps Will Go To," January 9, 2012, www.businessinsider.com/zappos-customer-service-crm-2012-1.
5. "The Good, The Bad and The Beautiful of Employee Empowerment," August 5, 2013, http://ritzcarltonleadershipcenter.com/2013/08/440/.

Chapter 10

1. "Lean manufacturing," https://en.wikipedia.org/wiki/Lean
   _manufacturing.
2. "Holacracy and Self-Organization," www.zapposinsights.com/about
   /holacracy.

Chapter 12

1. Jean M. Twenge, W. Keith Campbell, and Elise C. Freeman,
   "Generational Differences in Young Adults' Life Goals, Concern for
   Others, and Civic Orientation, 1966–2009," www.apa.org/pubs
   /journals/releases/psp-102-5-1045.pdf.
2. "Hillberg & Berk Jewelry," *Dragons' Den*, www.cbc.ca/dragonsden
   /pitches/hillberg-berk-jewelry.
3. Guy Kawasaki, *Enchantment: The Art of Changing Minds, Hearts, and
   Actions*, www.goodreads.com/quotes/701745-if-you-don-t-toot-your
   -own-horn-don-t-complain-that.

Chapter 14

1. See: www.facebook.com/workplace.
2. "The Ultimate List of Hiring Statistics For Hiring Managers, HR
   Professionals, and Recruiters," https://business.linkedin.com/content
   /dam/business/talent-solutions/global/en_us/c/pdfs/Ultimate-List-of
   -Hiring-Stats-v02.04.pdf.

INDEX